Beauty IN BROKENNESS
Transformed by Grace

TRETIA STEWART ANGUS

Published by

DAYELight
PUBLISHERS

ISBN: 978-1-958443-08-8 (paperback)

For speaking engagements, contact;
Tretia Stewart Angus
Kingdom Encounter Ministry International
Email:kingdom.encounter21@gmail.com

Scripture quotations marked "KJV" are taken from the Holy Bible, King James Version (Public Domain).

Lovingly dedicated to my wonderful family: my husband, Apostle Okino Angus, who is my anchor, support and prayer partner, confidante and friend; also my two daughters, Theamoy and Justine, who kept my head above water when I really wanted to quit.

"And the vessel that he made of clay was marred in the hand of the potter: so he made it again another vessel, as seemed good to the potter to make it." (Jeremiah 18:4 - KJV).

CONTENTS

PREFACE

A broken vessel may lose some of its ability to function according to its original design because it is impaired. Nevertheless, although its total functionality may be somewhat impaired, it is still a vessel and can be used to carry out its function to some degree, despite its flaws.

The story is told of the potter who decided to create a masterpiece. As the clay was placed on the potter's wheel to be fashioned into a beautiful vessel, it became marred in the potter's hand. As a master builder who is skillful at his work, instead of throwing the pieces of clay into the garbage, the potter placed it again on the wheel and began to fashion it into the vessel that he wanted. The potter was wise because he knew that no matter how many times the clay was broken, once it was in his hands, he could fashion it into a priceless masterpiece.

"Then I went down to the potter's house, and, behold, he wrought a work on the wheels. And the vessel that he made of clay was marred in the hand of the potter: so he made it again another vessel, as seemed good to the potter to make it." (Jeremiah 18:3-4 - KJV).

The words spoken by the Lord God to Jeremiah the prophet resonated with my spirit as I wrote because I was that vessel on the potter's wheel. **Beauty In Brokenness** is a true testament of the unwavering love of my Heavenly Father, demonstrated through Jesus Christ and endorsed by Holy Spirit, my Comforter and Friend.

Part One
The Beginning

"Train up a child in the way he should go: and when he is old, he will not depart from it." (Proverbs 22:6 - KJV).

November 15, 1976 heralded the birth of a beautiful baby girl. My parents decided to call me Tretia. I was the second of five siblings. Though premature at birth, my physical development was one where I transitioned from one stage of development to another through the watchful eyes of my mother, then my father.

Raising a premature child was quite a daunting task for my parents at some points because I was smaller and more susceptible to respiratory problems, which developed as I grew. God, in all His goodness, kept me safe from sicknesses that would normally endanger the life of a "preemie" baby.

I do not recall much of my early years living with my mother and father (both my parents had to fill me in where I needed clarity to write certain aspects of this book). My parents were living together in a "common law" relationship. They were young and inexperienced about many things, and life as it seemed then was rough. No child wants to see their parents separated because parents are the centre of a child's world. Little did I know that I was going to experience separation, anxiety and, in some instances, rejection because my father and mother decided to go their separate ways due to irreconcilable differences. This dealt a major blow and caused the family to split.

My older brother was sent to the country to live with his grandfather from my mother's side. My father, who loved me dearly, decided to raise me on his own because I was the eldest daughter and the second child. Therefore, I was back and forth visiting my mother and living with my father. This was where the hands of fate began to shape my life. At this crucial stage in my development, I was forced to choose between both parents. For the most part, my father took full responsibility for my upbringing so I was separated from my other siblings. This affected me greatly because I was forced to grow up like an only child. I was about three years old at that time.

According to Erikson's stages of development, I was at the second stage of early development; I was just learning independence. It was the stage of Autonomy versus Shame and Doubt. Erikson's theory concluded that at this stage the child needs support from parents so that repeated failures and ridicule are not the only experiences encountered. I therefore endorse the fact that parents need to encourage their child/children to become independent, whilst at the same time protecting the child so that constant failure is avoided. Hence, a delicate balance is required from both parents.

I lost trust in my mother (in my world, I thought she did not care) and even doubted her love for me. I drew closer to my father because he was the person I saw when I woke up during the night and the one who stood by me and took care of me when my mother had to leave **(this I will discuss in detail further in this book).** The fact that I was alone with my father most times helped me to develop a certain amount of independence which has resulted in me being able to assert myself a particular way in order to get things done. I learnt to do things on my own initiative, and my father was there to encourage me to do better.

At the age of three, I was enrolled in an early childhood institution where I began my early years of academic training. I was small in stature; hence, I was given the name "Sweeny." Nevertheless, I was famous for drawing the attention of adults with my "mature speech."

Single parenting is never an easy role to play, especially for a father. The constraint of being a carpenter and taking care of a small child was very demanding. However, it never daunted my father. He tried to bring some balance to my social, educational, and spiritual upbringing.

Although I was just a tiny tot, I could clearly remember my father getting me dressed for Sunday School every Sunday morning. I was attired in beautiful dresses that made me look smart. I would run to church, which was but a few feet away from where I lived. I would get lost in the merriment of singing my favourite "Sunday School Songs" and listening to "Bible Stories" that came to life through mesmerizing "role plays."

After church each Sunday, I would walk back to my house singing the songs I learnt in Sunday School or memorizing the scripture verses that I was taught.

As a believer in Christ Jesus, I could see the workings of the hand of God in my life from the beginning. Even though my father would not go to church, there was never a Sunday morning when I did not go, even when it rained. I now know that what I am, and who I am becoming in Christ, is as a result of the righteous seed that was planted in my spirit from a tender age. My earthly father was obedient to the tiny nudgings of the Holy Spirit to grow me in the fear of God. I can safely say that when you show a child the right pathway to take on the road of life, it will never be forgotten.

"But continue thou in the things which thou hast learned and hast been assured of, knowing of whom thou hast learned them; And that from a child thou hast known the holy scriptures, which are able to make thee wise unto salvation through faith which is in Christ Jesus." (2 Timothy 3:14-15 - KJV).

A child who has been taught godly principles and the ways of life through scripture will have a firm foundation on which to not only stand but remain grounded throughout his or her lifetime, despite adversities. The scripture expressly shows where Paul the Apostle encouraged his spiritual son, Timothy, to hold fast to the truths that he had learned because they were sound and able to make him wise (see 2 Timothy 1:13).

Who I am becoming in Christ is a result of the sound teaching I received while I was attending Sunday school as a child and in my teenage years. Such teaching is resonating in my spirit even now as an adult.

EARLY LEARNING

My educational journey began from conception. Some people may assume that the moment you start attending preschool is when you begin to learn. That is the furthest thing from the truth. From the moment a life comes into focus, learning is inevitable.

According to Pacific Lutheran University, research has shown that babies start learning a language while in their mothers' womb; about ten weeks before birth. In addition to that, Noam Chomski, a well-known behaviorist on language acquisition, theorized that children are born with an innate ability to learn and develop language very quickly. This, he assumes, is based on a Language Acquisition Device that nature has given to humans from conception.

With that said, I believe that even as I was in my mother's womb I was learning because sound travels in waves from the outside world to the foetus. From the moment I could understand human relation, language, sounds, and symbols, I had a yearning desire to learn. My mother told me that I was very inquisitive. I would ask a lot of questions, but I feared going into buildings. The fears I had of buildings developed when I was taken to the clinic for regular immunization and the nurse gave me an injection. I refused to go into any building from that time. Fear gripped me like a second skin! I would cry like the sky was falling on me. Therefore, I refused to go into any enclosed building because it reminded me of the nurse at the clinic.

Please note that no fear is of God. The Bible expressly states that:

"For God hath not given us the spirit of fear; but of power, and of love, and of a sound mind." (2 Timothy 1:7- KJV).

The enemy of our soul, the devil, has always tried to intercept us on our path of life. He tries to push his evil agenda on us through fear, sickness, and death. Even as a child I was infused with fear. I was fearful of pain and the unknown, but God, in all His love and care, was there to protect me, even from conception.

My dad realized that apart from Sunday School, I also needed a formal education. My early years of formal education began at Brother Reeves Early Childhood, which was not very far from where we were living. I was amazed at how beautiful the classroom appeared. There were handwritten charts with bold letters and bright colors which provided the print-rich environment I needed to stimulate my mind into learning. As such, reading became my hobby.

One evening, as I got home from school, my father presented me with a small book. I cannot vividly remember receiving any other gift from him before that, but it was the best gift I had ever received. It was a book of ABCs, with onset and rime, rhymes and jingles. Although the book was in black and white, it really did not make much of a difference. The pictures in the book popped out at me like a kaleidoscope of colors. The most interesting thing is that every evening when my father got home, he would put me on his lap and teach me how to read from the book. This was a big game changer. It revolutionized my thinking as it relates to the importance of education and learning to read, even at a tender age. I became one of the "top" readers and spellers in my class during my primary years.

There was a quest to know things. I had a thirst for knowledge, so I would read any book or written material that I got my hands on. I recall one specific book that my father had under a night table; it was a huge yellow-covered book entitled, "Book of Bible Stories." That book became my best friend. The colorful pictures jumped out at me as I read it from cover to cover. I did not mind whenever my father had to go out on errands because I would lie on the floor and read Bible stories for hours. Soon after, boredom began to set in, and I was reading the same story over and over again. I became a "detective" and began combing the house for evidence of hidden books.

One day I had a hunch to lift the mattress off the bed. So I went to one of the corners, and with all the strength I could exert, I lifted the mattress. It was like I had hit the jackpot and my budding detective skills paid off because I saw several picture magazines. I took out one of the magazines, and I had never seen anything like it before. There were not many words, but it had lots of pictures of handsome men and beautiful women who were scantily clad. My little heart began pounding faster than I could possibly imagine. Deep down in the pit of my stomach I felt like I was doing something wrong. Furthermore, the books were hidden. If they wanted me to see them, the books would be out in the open.

My interest was piqued as I scanned the content of the "eye-popping" magazine. I sat on the floor beside the bed and read through every page of the magazine. When I was through reading, I tried to return each picture book to its "safe zone" not wanting anyone to know I was reading them. In my mind I never for one minute thought of telling my parents about the books I saw. I knew they were not for my dad, but they belonged to one of my "in-laws." Day after day I would read and scan through the pornographic material, not realizing the devastating effect it was having on my psychological well-being.

As cited by an online source, "Pornography is harmful to children of all ages!" Furthermore, it must be noted that there are adverse effects for those who are caught up in its web. Research ultimately shows that: "Children or adolescents may experience autonomic sexual arousal at the sight of pornography, which can confuse them into thinking they 'like' what they see, when in fact their bodies are reacting instinctively without the 'approval' of their brain."

It cannot be overstated how much parents want to raise healthy children who are mentally and emotionally stable. Consequently, when children are exposed to sexually explicit material like books, magazines, and even television, it most times heightens their need to get involved and desensitizes them to moral decay that often sets in.

Parents can give support to their child/children exposed to pornography by following these few simple steps:

- Earn your child's trust and get him or her to talk about what they see.
- Stay calm; this will alleviate the fear of the child thinking he or she is to be blamed.
- Listen intently without interrupting.

19

- Never give your child a lecture.
- Allow the child to feel comfortable talking with you by not making him or her feel guilty.
- Give place to self-expression. It allows the child to talk honestly and openly about how he or she feels.
- Talk about sex and educate your child but not in one go; give them time to absorb the information.
- If you are a Christian, pray with your child.
- Get cooperate Christian counseling. Based on how exposed the child is, expert advice may be needed.
- Be a friend, so your child can feel comfortable talking with you about anything.[1]

The eyes are like windows to the soul; whatever the eyes look on, whether good or bad, will affect the soul and also your thought process. The eyes are also the light of the soul and also that which we use to see the world around us. If your eyes become dark, then you are unable to see. Whatever the eyes see continuously will at some point become the focal point on which the mind rests.

Can you imagine a child between the ages of four and six being completely engrossed in reading pornographic materials at his or her own leisure, without the knowledge of a responsible adult?

---

[1] https://preventchildabuse.org/resource/understanding-the-effects-of-pornography-on-children/ Retrieved April 24, 2020

I was that child; life was like a ticking time bomb, and no one knew how dangerous it was for me to be living in my skin and in my mind during that period. An inquisitive mind is good when you are learning in accordance with what is an acceptable standard for a child. However, when it is focusing on the wrong things, then it is dangerous.

EARLY SOCIAL LIFE

I was the second of three children for my parents. My brother, who was the eldest, went to live with his grandparents by my mother's side when my parents separated, but my sister, who was the youngest at the time, lived with my mother. The separation of my parents did not allow me to see my siblings on a regular basis, only on holidays and some weekends.

I can clearly remember how burdensome it was, even though I was young, the thought of not being able to play and interact with my other siblings. It left me feeling lonely, sometimes rejected, and even angry. I would often wonder why things were the way they were. Nevertheless, I would play by myself in my father's work space. I familiarized myself with all the tools he used in carpentry because on certain days when he was home working, he would ask me to assist him by finding the tools he needed for the job at hand. I took great pride in my father's work by making myself available amidst playing intermittently in the saw dust from the lumber he was cutting.

My father was living in a sparsely populated community in Denbigh. At that time there were neighbours with children, and on rare occasions, I would get a chance to play with them.

Separate and apart from Shwana*[2] and her sisters, my only other close neighbor was an elderly gentleman, Mass Sydney. He was a returning resident from England, very kind, good-natured, and friendly. When my father was going out on the weekend, maybe to the market or to get a job done, he would leave me at Mass Sydney's house. I was elated whenever I got a chance to go to his home because I would eat until my stomach was full. Not only that, but my mouth would also water for the custard apple ice cream that he would make.

---

[2] *Not her real name.

Part Two
Sexual Abuse: When It All Began

"No matter how difficult life seems, people with a past need to make their way to Jesus. Regardless of the obstacles within and without, they must reach Him." —T.D. Jakes

WHAT IS SEXUAL ABUSE?

According to the American Psychological Association, "sexual abuse is any unwanted sexual activity, with perpetrators using force, making threats or taking advantage of victims not able to give consent."

Many of our children are and have been suffering and maimed and sometimes even lose their lives because of sexual abuse. This is a present evil that has plagued the lives of different families from various stratums of society; the rich, the poor, and the in between. In my estimation, and from my own reservoir of experiences, at least one child in every household experience sexual abuse. Since most victims feel threatened and are often frightened and fearful of the outcome, they normally choose to remain silent. Thus, the offense may go unnoticed or swept under the carpet because of the fear, embarrassment, and shame that families and even the victims may encounter.

All forms of abuse against children are criminal acts against the rights of a child and must be brought to the fore and given strict attention because the implications can be devastating, especially for the victim and family.

Sexual abuse is devastating because it interferes with every aspect of human life, namely: physical, emotional, psychological, spiritual, and affective domain of a child's development. This violent, inhumane act knows no creed, class, or gender. This is an immoral act that weighs heavily on any individual who is or was exposed to and violated by perpetrators who want only to force himself/herself on a victim.

I took the time out to pen the scenes of my life in such a manner that will lay a foundation for you to understand that your future does not have to look like your past. Even though there were terrible bumps, bruises, potholes, stops, and turns in my life, it never stopped the hand of God from reaching me. Jesus is able to meet you wherever you are. When there was no one for me to talk to, no one saw the agony and pain I had to endure, Jesus was there, waiting patiently for me to cry out to Him. I cried out to Him in my distress and He heard me and delivered me from all my fears (see Psalm 18:6). Jesus can deliver you!

The earliest memory I have of sexual molestation was in my pre-school years. I still have questions that are unanswered, such as "Why did you do it?" and "Who or what drove you to hurt a child?"

As was mentioned in **Part One**, I spent most of my early childhood and part of my primary years with my father. He had the awesome responsibility of taking care of me, most times single-handedly.

It was summer, so father decided to take me to my mother to spend the holiday. I was excited and fearful all at the same time. I was happy because I would get a chance to bond with my other sibling. Tika*[3] was two years younger than me, and it was a great opportunity to have some fun time since her weekend visits to my father were cut short because of school. What I did not know was that fatal summer would be the beginning of many horrific experiences.

I was cruelly introduced to sexual abuse. It was one of the most horrendous experiences I can recall as a child. At that time, I was around four years of age and still in pre-school. My cousin Keera*[4], who was living with mother at the time, was the "devil's agent" in disguise. I did not know this until I had the most horrendous experience.

It was a day like no other, and my mother had to go to work. One particular morning, for some strange reason, I was horrified when I saw her leave. I just did not want her to leave us that day. In my heart, I just wished she would stay home. Little did I know that it was my subconscious picking up on something diabolic.

After my mother left, all I can recall was Keera and Tika going under the bed. Keera was the eldest among us. I had no ill feeling that she was up to something naughty, so I followed suit and went under the bed. I thought we would be playing hide-and-go-seek or some fun game.

As I went underneath the bed, Tika asked me to take off my panties. In my little mind, I was puzzled. I could hear my heart beating as loud as a drum in my ears. Something was not

---

[3] *Not her real name.
[4] *Not her real name.

adding up. Keera told me to lay on my back and she opened my legs, while Tika was looking on. Keera then inserted something that looked like a piece of stick, then an old rusty nail into my vagina. Pain like I have never experienced ripped through and pierced my fragile body. It felt like a thousand thorns ripping into my flesh and I was going to black out. I began howling in pain as tears ran down my face. She took a piece of cloth and stuffed it into my little mouth, gagging me and almost rendering me breathless. I could not cry; she threatened to hurt me even more if I cried. She then sat back and watched me bleed while my younger sibling was looking on. When she did not feel satisfied, she urinated in a container and told me to drink it. When I refused to drink the urine, she beat me on my naked upturned bottom with a piece of coconut tree branch which she had brought into the room and placed under the bed. The pain was so unbearable that I became numb after a while.

Keera threatened to beat me if I told my mother anything, so I kept it all to myself. I walked in fear daily and dreaded the moment when my mother would leave me again with my evil cousin. I suffered in silence and fear. Keera hated me; she was like the devil in human form. I was so afraid of even looking at her. It was the worst time of my life, and no one knew about it. I just tucked the horrifying experience deep in my mind and pretended like nothing happened.

WHAT ARE THE IMPLICATIONS/CONSEQUENCES OF CHILD SEXUAL ABUSE?

My experience as an educator, minister, and counselor, as well as research, has shown that sexual abuse may have adverse symptomatic effects on a child at each stage of development. Some of these effects may be psychological, physical, emotional, and cognitive. This may have severe consequences on the process of development in the life of the child, family, school, community, and society at large. Everyone is affected by this evil; no one is exempted. Therefore, each person in the circle of life must play his or her part to rid society of this unnecessary evil that has plagued humanity since ancient times. These are some negative effects of child sexual abuse, which include but are not limited to:

- Guilt
- Shame
- Low self-esteem
- Self-loathing
- Rejection
- Sexual immorality
- Multiple sex partners
- Teenage pregnancy
- Fear of relationships
- Running away from home
- Post-Traumatic Stress Disorder
- Alcohol/Drug Abuse
- Poor academic performance
- Suicidal thoughts/attempted suicide
- Sexually transmitted or blood-borne infections

NOTE TO PARENTS

It is imperative that you spend quality time with your child or children. Get to know them and watch out for tell-tale signs of any form of abuse. Children must be comfortable talking with their parents even more than they talk with their friends. Even though most parents often strive to be first disciplinarians, they must also strike a balance where being a friend to their child or children is paramount. In this way, children will not feel fearful of sharing secrets with a parent or caregiver, especially when that child's safety is compromised.

It is often said that the closest person to an individual or family is the one who will hurt or harm them. I believe this is true based on my experience. Oftentimes a child's life is endangered, and parents are not aware because they may have absolute trust in family members, who are left to take care of younger children. If it had not been for the Lord on my side, I would have died. Although it did not seem that way in the beginning, I know the Lord had set angels to watch over and keep me from that time onwards.

I must give thanks to God for keeping me through the abusive episodes in my life. In part one, I stated that the hand of God was there in my life, and quite evident as far back as I can remember. It is easy for me to talk about my life in detail because I know the Lord has delivered me from the snares, fears, and traps of the enemy.

The devil is always trying to override and rewrite the blueprint for your life by trying to superimpose his evil plans over God's great plan. The enemy of our souls wants us to believe his lies that our Heavenly Father does not care for us, but might I remind you from scripture according to the book Jeremiah:

"For I know the thoughts that I think toward you, saith the Lord, thoughts of peace, and not of evil, to give you an expected end." (Jeremiah 29:11- KJV).

I was meditating on this verse of scripture during my quest for answers when it was revealed to me that the same way God has a plan for your life, for you to prosper and be in good health, the devil has also mapped out an evil plan to throw us totally off-balance from the will and purposes of God. He tries to ensnare us in his evil trap.

HOW DOES HE CARRY OUT HIS TASK?

The devil is not omnipresent. In order to carry out his evil onslaught on humanity, he uses demonic entities, animals and human agents to kill our purpose, steal our joy, and destroy our God-given destinies.

There are demonic agents on assignment, set out to destroy the purpose of God in your life. Oftentimes the enemy seeks to carry out this plan by trying to plant a seed from we were in our mother's womb. You see, the old adversary is a master planner, and if he cannot get you while you are in the womb, he then waits until the time of your birth.

This can be seen in the life of Jesus, where in Matthew 2, Herod the King told the wise men to search for baby Jesus and bring back word to him once they have found Him. King Herod was only carrying out the plan of Satan. The diabolical plan of the devil was to kill the Saviour of the world in an attempt to stop humanity from receiving eternal life through Jesus Christ.

When I look back on all the crazy things that have happened in my life, I recognize that people were being used as demonic portals and guest houses to carry out an evil plan that was designed to kill, steal and destroy a soul destined for greatness in God and Christ.

SILENCE SCREAMS

They say that "Silent river runs deep." It is often said, "the things that you don't say won't hurt you," but I beg to differ; what you don't say will hurt you.

Every child has a right to be able to speak and be heard. I never knew that was true or that it applied to me. I never felt that what I had to say was important, and I was to be blamed for anything that happened to me.

Parents of the past era had the audacity to say, "Children must be seen and not heard." I was unable to relate to my parents how I thought or felt about any given situation. I suffered in silence and pain for most of my life. Thoughts of suicide plagued my mind. "I'd rather die than live to face another day," were the words that echoed from the silence that screamed at me.

No one knew, and no one heard the loud screams that echoed from the silence that permeated my life. I was always quiet, but that was no reason to believe life was fine and dandy or that I was happy. Little did my family, parents, teachers, or friends know about the burden, shame, guilt, and fear that engulfed me.

I never spoke to anyone about the horrible things that I was going through as a child; I remained silent. Fear gripped me to the point where I suffered in silent agony, although inside I screamed like a siren with the desire to talk to someone in order to unburden my mind. I was just a kid. There was no one I could trust so the books I read offered a temporary escape from the horrors of my childhood fears. In a matter of hours, I would read two books at most. I felt trapped and imprisoned in the cage of my mind. My only route of escape was the novels that I continued to read on a daily basis.

As far as I can allow my mind to stretch, there was always some form of abuse that perpetuated my life. I wondered why I was experiencing this and why no one knew; or was it that no one cared enough to take a second look.

The onslaught of the physical and sexual abuse from those who should protect me left me wounded and scarred physically, academically, emotionally, and psychologically. My life took a downward spiral because it seemed like my inner scars were unseen to the human eye but attracted the most perverted souls to my life.

The early pre-school years in the life of a child are a very crucial stage in a child's development. This stage of development is known as the initiative versus guilt, as theorized by Erikson.

At this stage of my development, I was quite aware of the widening social world. It was even more challenging for me because I had little to no trust in those who were my caregivers because of their lustful and perverted mindset toward me.

SILENT AS A LAMB TO THE SLAUGHTER

There was no stability in my life; one moment I was with my father, and the next I was with some stranger, stepmother, or family member.

My father traveled extensively. For more than half of the year, he was in a foreign land working; furthermore, he was a carpenter. My father had to rely on other caregivers to take care of me so that he could earn some money.

One of my stepmothers, Claudine*[5] (now deceased), had the privilege of taking care of me. She lived in an extended family so the household was large; it was a "big yard."

My summer holidays were now centred on Claudine's family. Her mother was a Bible-believing Christian, so a part of my summer holidays was spent in Vocation Bible School. I had a deep desire for church and the things of God even as a child. I looked forward to those times with great expectation not knowing that God was using those moments, though I had a myriad of bad experiences, to curve me into my destiny.

The Christmas season brought fun and more fun with us baking and cooking. I was comfortable because the family took care

---

[5] *Not her real name.

of me. My discomfort came when two of her brothers, on separate occasions, molested me.

I started to believe it was a normal part of life growing up. I was not yet in my teens, but I began to indulge in foreplay and started to desire having my body touched.

There were moments when I initiated sexual contact because I thought it was a normal thing to do. I stopped feeling guilty and gave into the fantasies plaguing my mind. All through my ordeals, no one knew what I was going through. I was as silent as a lamb.

In my early years as a child, my life was overwhelmed with guilt. I told myself that I deserved all the bad things that were happening to me. The fact is, no one would believe me and, furthermore, it was too shameful to talk about. I was undoubtedly afraid to tell anyone. What would father or mother think of me? They would punish me and tell everyone about it; so I thought.

It was the time of my life when I had to assume responsibility for my own life and behaviour.

FIRST ENCOUNTER WITH DEATH

We were alone at home one day, and mother told Keera to cook dinner, which she did reluctantly. She was inside the house doing something and asked me to go into the kitchen and take the pot off the stove. Being fearful of her and not wanting to incur her wrath, I hastily went to the kitchen and removed the pot from the stove. The door leading from the kitchen to the dining area was not open, so I had to walk on the outside with the pot in my hand. I took my time and walked gingerly towards the front door, with my head down and paying close attention to the pot in my hand because I did not want to spill the food as it would mean a night without dinner.

Keera was standing in the doorway but I never saw her, so I accidentally bumped into her. The pot of rice somehow burned her on her leg as it fell out of my hand. I was so frightened I opened my mouth in shock and disbelief.

Keera was furious; she picked me up by my two feet and dropped me squarely on my head. The yard was filled with sharp rocks and stones so there was no cushion for the fall. I fell with a loud thud on my head. I was out for a few seconds. When I opened my eyes, I felt something warm trickling down my face. I cannot recall clearly what happened afterward because I blacked out for a while.

I regained consciousness after some time had passed; by this time it was a bit dark. Keera got some ointment and squeezed it into the open wound. There was a deep gash on the right side of my forehead. She tried to disguise the gaping hole in my forehead by putting more ointment in it. Again, I was threatened not to tell my mother what happened. I wondered if someone could be so evil. I never offended Keera; I was only visiting my mother for a short time but for some unknown reason my cousin hated my guts, and I was terrified.

Mother came home late from work that evening; however, I was already sleeping. Keera gave mom a made-up story. "She stubbed her toe on a stone and fell," that was her story.

I had a high fever during the night; no doubt the wound was infected by bacteria. Early the next morning my mother had to take me to the doctor. The wound was so bad they had to keep me for observation. The doctors and nurses questioned me to find out what happened. I thought about it and told them the same story Keera gave my mother. They cleaned the wound and sutured it before discharging me from the hospital sometime later. I was so afraid of Keera that I could not tell my mother the truth about what happened. I suffered in silence, and my little heart grew cold and bitter towards Keera. Not long after, my mother found out she was lying and sent her back to her other family. The holiday ended, and I went back to my father.

I do not know how I managed to pull through. I believe that God had His hand on my life even at a tender age. He preserved my steps and delivered me from the clutches of the enemy. That encounter with Keera was meant to kill me, but God rescued me from the angry jaws of death.

Hurt people, often if not always, hurt other people if past issues are not dealt with in a professional, orderly, and timely manner. For years I walked with the pain of what Keera did to me as a child, and yes, the scars are still there. The scars are there to an extent because I did not have the parental support I needed at the time, not only to believe me but to ensure I received the necessary care and counseling needed to hurdle such a traumatic experience. I was often beaten for no apparent reason, had my hands and feet bounded, and then placed in a nest of ants. These tiny creatures made a meal of me. My screams for help apparently fuelled her sick desires to be avenged from the torture of a past I knew nothing about.

SECOND ENCOUNTER WITH DEATH: A DAY I WILL NEVER FORGET

When it got difficult for my father to take care of me by himself, he sent me to live with my mother permanently.

I was in my early teenage years, and the onset of puberty was evident in my developing body. I was maturing more rapidly than my mother could realize. I had quite a curvaceous body and womanhood was quite evident, even at fourteen years of age.

Seeing that I am the second child and the eldest daughter of both my parents, most of the home duties and chores were my responsibility. My mother had to work in order to give support to five children who were still going to school. Even though I was in my early adolescent years, I had the responsibility of taking care of the home and four other siblings while my mother and step-father worked.

I vividly remember running some errands for my mother one day. I had to go to the grocery store in May Pen and public transportation was the only means of getting to my destination quickly. So I boarded a small bus at my gate and set off on my journey to the grocery store. On my way home from the supermarket I got into a small mini-van; it was packed from front to back so I had to stand while the adults sat; that was the routine then.

As I stood in the over-loaded mini-van, I became aware that someone was looking at me rivetingly. My gaze caught hold of a handsome gentleman with a clean shaved face and bold but sneaky eyes. He seemed to be in his early thirties. A nervousness came over me and I started feeling oddly uncomfortable because he was aware that I had caught his eyes. A few minutes after that weird encounter, I got off at my gate, which was close to the main road.

A few days later, there was an encounter in my yard with a police officer and a little boy who was living close by. Shaun*[6] was about three years old and his father was not home so he ran out on the road and a police officer was just in time to see him, so they came over to the house to investigate. To my surprise, it was the same gentleman from the mini-van who was staring me down a few days before. He was a police officer.

He quizzed me on the whereabouts of Shaun's father, and I told him. His tone was threatening, and I almost felt like I was in trouble. Shaun usually came by the house in the evenings. I would feed him if he was hungry or give him a bath if he was dirty. Later in the evening his father would come for him. I informed the officer of the daily routine, but he seemed not to be satisfied. The police officer began interrogating me about my family, which I told him willingly. He finally left the house, and I went back to complete my daily chores.

---

[6] *Not his real name.

The house that we occupied was a small two-bedroom with two other unfinished rooms. My siblings and I were quite comfortable even though we had to use a bathroom which was detached from the house. There were no burglar bars on the house, just regular glass Louvre windows. It was a quiet community. We were surrounded by neighbours so we felt safe.

It was a normal Friday evening and my mother had to work late again, but that did not stop the flow at home. I took care of my siblings like an adult was there. We all ate dinner and turned in for bed. On this particular night, I decided to sleep by myself in one of the unfinished rooms, which was very close to the room that was occupied by my other siblings.

Around 1:00 a.m., I woke up suddenly because I thought I heard a sound in the other unfinished room. I thought it was my mind or I was dreaming so I went back to sleep. About an hour later I was rudely awakened by a nudge. Someone was standing over my bed. I slowly woke out of sleep and raised my body off the bed; my eyes encountered something that looked like a gun, and it was. My eyes went to the face of the individual holding the gun. It was the policeman.

I could not believe what was happening to me. I heard the heavy breathing of my mother sleeping, and I started shaking. The man with the gun looked down at me and whispered in my ears, "If yuh move or scream, mi kill you." While speaking, I heard the click of the gun. He then told me to come with him. I told him he would have to kill me because I was not going anywhere with him. He pushed the gun in my head. I was shaking like a leaf on a tree. My mind was spinning like a top; fear gripped me. I shakily told him to allow me to go put on my shoes and some clothes and I will go with him. He then let me go and I slipped into the other room. I went straight under the bed. I could hear my heart pounding like it was leaping out of my chest.

I prayed for day to break. What was going to happen? Where was this man? What would my mother and step-father think? Will he kill us all? Those were the questions that swam around in my head while my heart was beating frantically like a loud off-key drum. I heard the rooster crowing and morning broke. Everyone was in one piece, but I was a total wreck. I was alive; I escaped death yet again. I could not speak; no one knew the horror I endured the night before. The only tell-tale sign that something happened and I was not dreaming was the fact that the back door to the kitchen was left open. Yet again I remained silent. I was too afraid to talk to anyone about what I was going through. I felt ashamed and embarrassed about the way my life was turning out.

PART THREE
HIGH SCHOOL YEARS

I attended a prominent high school in Clarendon. Every morning I would walk to the bus stop to get the early bus for school. Being tardy for school was my worst fear as the principal, Mr. Griffiths, was a stickler for time. He would stand at the gate during the mornings to discipline the students who were repeatedly late and also to inspect their uniforms to ensure they were appropriately attired. One morning I forgot my school tie and, to my own demise, the principal stood at the foyer inspecting every student. He looked at me sternly and called me out of the line. My heart pounded in my chest like a judge's gavel. I knew then that I would feel the wrath of his belt, and I did. I never left home again without being completely attired for school.

The first and second years in high school were the best years of my school life. I did well academically and was able to remain in the A-stream classes. The batch of students in the year 1989 was the first set of Common Entrance students and I was in that batch.

I was not a sociable person, but I had a few friends who I was able to share thoughts and laugh with. I soon forgot the troubled years of my life but then something happened that shook my world and almost turned it upside-down. As I mentioned previously, I was living with my mother, stepfather, and siblings. My mother worked extremely long and hard; therefore, most times she did not get in until the wee hours of the morning (she was operating a bar and restaurant).

During the evenings when I got home from school, I would cook dinner so my younger siblings could eat as well as my stepfather and mother. Occasionally, my stepfather would cook because he liked to cook. One evening his nephew, Tom, came to look for him; they both cooked and we had a belly full. Tom was going to stay the night. He was young and quite athletic. He liked to watch Kung Fu and he would often show off his martial arts skills using his hands and feet skillfully. I always enjoyed Tom's company because he was always giving silly jokes that made my sister and me laugh.

As the evening was coming to an end and the sky began to darken, we all went inside to sit around the table. My stepfather and Tom began drinking red wine. I asked for some of the wine and they were hesitant to give it to me, but nevertheless, Tom brought a cup and poured some of the wine in it for me. Everything got blurry after I began drinking the wine. The only thing I remembered seeing was some white powder at the bottom of the cup. I asked my step-father what was in the cup, and he took it from me muttering to himself. In the meantime, Tom drew closer and his whole friendly demeanor changed and something else emerged.

Paul, my stepfather, had excused himself from the table, so Tom had enough time to speak to me. His arguments became sensual as he was trying to persuade me to talk to him about my boyfriend and sexual encounters. I was quite offended and began having an uneasy feeling in the pit of my stomach. I am not sure if Paul knew that his nephew was trying to molest me; he never said a word to me or asked me if I was okay. From that time onward, Tom would constantly provoke me or even try to force me to lay with him.

Those moments of pressure I endured were the worst times of my life. I felt like a rat that was trapped by a cat and there was nowhere to run. The thought of suicide came to mind several times because I thought it was the best way to end my constant run-ins with perverted men. To make things worse, my stepfather, who was always playful and kind, became very abusive. He would curse and swear if I did not complete a chore. As soon as my mother got home from work, he was always telling her some story about me. That always resulted in me getting a flogging from my mother. Most of the time, the stories were only half true. I hated this man because of what he was doing.

One day my siblings and I, along with our stepfather, were playing hide and go seek. Paul was jovial and spent time talking or playing with my sisters and me when my mother had to work. It was my time to hide so I went hiding in the partial darkness of the evening. Paul was the one searching for us. He came to where I was hiding and to my surprise, he held on to me and tried kissing me on the lips. I was shocked from my head to my toes. I refused to get caught up in that which he was trying to instigate. How could life treat me so unkind? I ran out of my hiding place and the game ended.

There was an invisible war being fought; there was a diabolic game being played in the dark realm for my soul. That incident and others led to some things even more drastic. I was like a broken jar, shattered into many pieces.

MENTAL BREAKDOWN

There were many grotesque and unsightly things happening around me. My home was not safe anymore. The people around me, who were supposed to protect me, could not be trusted. A heavy weight of sorrow, regret, and burden weighed me down. I was carrying so much baggage, and there was no one who saw it. There was no one who I felt comfortable enough to talk with. At nights I would hear my name being called, and when I answered, there was no one in the house with me. I would see images of my stepfather on my bed at night masturbating. I was not sure what was real or if I was hallucinating. I became forgetful so much so that my siblings started teasing me and calling me a liar because I would misplace items, and when asked about it, I told my mother I did not touch her things.

There were days when I had headaches; the pain I felt cannot be compared to any other pain I have had. My head would beat consistently for hours, like a double bass drum. It got so bad that one morning I woke from my sleep and could not take two steps without falling. My head became unstable on my body, and my limbs were droopy like that of a rag doll. I remember I started to vomit, and my body became lifeless. I passed out for a while. When I regained consciousness, I was at Doctor Dawes office on Manchester Avenue in May Pen. At this point, I cannot recall what the doctor told my mother, but one thing I know is that he told her it was something psychological. I was in second form at that time. The breakdown I encountered not only robbed me of my memory, but I was confined at home for about two to three months—that was almost one term out of school. No one knew the story behind the physical and mental

45

breakdown I suffered. It was another opportunity for the devil to kill me, but he could not because purpose must be birthed through my life on Earth.

Destiny was calling my name. I had to live; it was not my time to die. There is a God-given assignment on my life, and I am tied to it, so death had to back off.

Many of our young people are faced with similar challenges or situations and even worse. Let us as caregivers, teachers, ministers, and pastors, take our young people not just at face value or take them for granted, but seek to know their story and do our best to help. Sometimes they just need a friend to talk to. As people of God and Kingdom citizens, let us not close our eyes but ask the Spirit of God to endow us with wisdom and discernment so we will be able to see the "quiet ones" who are hurting deeply, so we can help them and save a life before it is too late.

One evening I did not go home; I went to one of my friend's house. Opal and I attended the same high school. Although she was an upper-grade student, we became friends. Leaving school and taking the bus to Opal's home was a temporary relief from the dark memories of my past that clawed at my conscience. I was trying to break free from the deep darkness that overshadowed my mind. It really did not bother me that my parents did not know where I was, and I did not care. I wanted to run away; I wanted to be the happy little girl who was not imprisoned, locked in a cage of worries, doubt, and fear.

There were days when I did not want to go home because I did not want to repeat the horrors of previous days. I would deliberately walk out into the busy thoroughfare so I could get mowed down by an incoming vehicle. All I thought of was death. One day my sister had to push me out of the road and save me from being hit by a truck. Life became unbearable and I did not want to live. At that point in time I began to scream at my mother, throw tantrums, and became quite unsubmissive. This infuriated her, and she lashed out at me by punishing me severely. What my mother did not realize was that I was trying to say something else to her, but she could not hear me. I further went on to tell my mother pointedly that my stepfather was not only lying and being physically abusive, but he was also sexually molesting me.

Shock and unbelief registered on her face as she pointedly told me it could not be true. Betrayal and rejection never felt worse; my mother refused to believe me. I could not swallow, and neither was I able to breathe. The only thing that came to mind was for that man to die. I became bitter, angry, and resentful.

That particular year, when it was time to transition to the third form, I flunked most of my exams and was demoted to a B-stream class. I was very disappointed in my academic performance. I still could not tell my teachers or even the guidance counselor why I was performing so poorly in school.

During the time of my placement in third form, I met Jenise. Jenise was a Bible-believing individual and I admired her for her calm composure and friendly demeanor. We started hanging out together during our morning and lunch break. As we talked about our likes and dislikes, I recognized that we had a lot in common. Our personalities, though opposite, seemed to complement each other. Jenise became my best and only friend in high school. Most of the time, if we were not studying or sharing ideas, we were exchanging our favourite novel because we both liked reading. Reading became a hobby, so when I was not in the art and craft department or under an almond tree, you would find us in the music room because those areas were quiet; far from the hustle and bustle of school life.

Doing Things My Own Way

"A man's heart deviseth his way: but the LORD directeth his steps." *(Proverbs 16:9 - KJV).*

It was in the summer of 1994 when I graduated from high school; I was seventeen years old. I left my father's home to go back and live with my mother (I went back to live with my father before leaving high school because of my stepfather). I was reluctant to leave my father's house because I did not get along with my mother. Nevertheless, I left because my stepmother insisted that I do so. The reason for this was because I had a boyfriend, and she did not want to be blamed for anything she thought might happen to me in the absence of my father, who migrated on a seasonal basis to work in Canada.

Living with my mother was not a bed of roses. The relationship with her was a bit strained. She did not know that I blamed her for all the bad things that happened to me as a child and even in my teenage years. My mother was always working so I had limited time to bond and connect with her in a mother-to-daughter relationship. I never knew what it felt like to get a hug or hear the words "I love you" from my mother when I was just a child. I thought long and hard about those things.

There was so much anger and resentment in my heart towards my mother. She seemed so rough at all times; a strict disciplinarian. Her authoritarian disposition as a parent did not lend itself to having a friendly conversation with her children. It was always discipline first; nothing else mattered. In her heart I knew she loved her children, but we could not tell by looking at her.

Unresolved issues and pent-up emotions got the better of me because I did not know what to do in my times of crisis. I needed my mother to listen to me, but I just did not know how to approach her.

Mother and I, we were always in a constant tussle, which led to us getting into a fight one day. I felt like that was the last straw.

As a young adult I was quite independent so I started making plans for my future. I knew for sure that I wanted a family of my own, one that had stability and love. Friends were not on my to-do list because I trusted no one. This mistrust came about because my only friend, Jenise*[7], betrayed me by sleeping with my then boyfriend, Ben. Little did I know that it was my cue to get out of the relationship.

---

[7] *Not her real name.

My mind was zooming in on an exclusive relationship, but I was searching for love in the wrong places and people. Ben was a charmer, a smooth talker. He had the right words and knew exactly what to say. I fell for his charms and forgave him for sleeping with my bestie.

Life was going okay, or so I thought. In my mind I knew what I wanted; a family. It was my decision to become pregnant, but Ben did not know this was my plan. I manipulated the whole process. Even though I was outside of Christ, I know now He was watching over me, and He never took His eyes off me.

I pause at this moment to tell you, dear reader, that the eyes of the Lord are on you; He watches over you. You may have broken covenant with the Lord and walked out of His will. He has not forgotten you. God is able to turn your mess into a message and use your past as a highway for those who are hurting to cross over into the Kingdom.

I broke covenant with the Lord; I stopped going to church. I never kept my end of the bargain. In a previous chapter, I mentioned how I cried out to the Lord in my distress (like the psalmist David), and He heard me and delivered me from all my fears. My vow to the Lord was that I would serve Him for the rest of my life if He took me out of the abusive situation I was in. God is always faithful, but I never kept my end of the bargain. I set out to have things my way, which was the wrong way (I know that now). Never make a vow you do not intend to keep.

When I decided to have a baby, I was just out of high school. Sometimes in our lives, as young adults, we make some foolish choices. I never counted the cost; never knew I would pay dearly and almost with my life. The thing is, I thought I was hurting my mother. I was being rebellious trying to get back at her. I wanted her to know I was a woman, and she could not run my life.

When mother found out I was pregnant with twins and living under her roof, it was like I made the worst mistake in the history of mankind. I was on my own. I had to leave the house.

I spent most of the pregnancy with Ben's parents in the country. It was during this time that I went into labour. I was only in my second trimester (six months pregnant). It was a long drive from the country to get to the May Pen Hospital. I was all the way in Brandon Hill, close to Kellits. The stress of the pregnancy and all that was happening with my mother got the better of me. My blood pressure kept falling, so I believe that pushed me into early labour.

All this time, Ben and his family were the only family I knew. My father had nothing to do with me. When he found out I was pregnant, he told me, in no uncertain terms, how worthless I was. The relationship with my family was null and void; I felt like a cast out. This was a stressful period in my life. I developed asthma in that period of time, and it was only the grace and mercy of God that kept me going. I had no friend, no one to share with, and no one to talk to. I resigned to doing what I did best; suffer in silence.

At about 4:00 a.m., I was at the May Pen Hospital in pain. This was in the month of October in the year 1995. I had a high-risk pregnancy; one of the twins was in a breached position. This meant that the second baby would come out feet first. I felt excruciating, mind-numbing pain like I never had in my life. I prayed, "Lord, forgive me of my sins." The first baby was born; she came out blue and was rushed to the incubator. For another hour the second baby struggled to come through the birth canal. When she finally came out, she was not breathing; both babies were placed in an incubator, and there was a slim chance that they would survive.

As I lay in the delivery room, many thoughts flooded my mind. Why would God allow me to go through so much pain, give birth and then allow the babies to die? This was a nagging question in my mind. I never had a clue or an answer for that question, but now that I am older and wiser, I understand that God has a blueprint for my life and I was the one who deviated from the plan to do my own thing. But GOD! In all His sovereignty, goodness and mercy snatched me from the burning inferno. Hallelujah!

You are not too far gone, my friend, where Jesus Christ cannot reach down His blood-stained hands to hold you. He did it just for me, and He will do it for you. Believe!

Both babies died; they were unable to breathe on their own. I walked away from the hospital empty and broken. I felt ridiculed and rejected by my family. I did not want to face them, so arrangements were made for me to stay with my aunt in Osbourne Store. Aunt J agreed so I left the hospital and went straight to her home. My Aunt J, who was quite compassionate, welcomed me into her home. She was at home with me as I grieved, not just for the loss of the babies but for how my family treated me. No one called or came to see me.

It was a time in my life when I went to the lowest of the low. Depression was my meal morning, noon, and night. I cried for what seemed an eternity. I felt death creeping upon me several times. I remember one day my aunt walked into the room as I felt my body falling into a deep slumber. My feet were lifeless, and my speech became slurred. Aunt J, who was a backslider, started praying loudly. She rebuked the spirit of death, and I regained consciousness. During that time of mourning, I decided to commit my life to the Lord. I was not going to church, but right there in my room I began to pray and ask the Lord to keep me. As I prayed daily, read my Bible, and sought the Lord, He brought comfort to my heart. The ache in my heart subsided as I reached out to the Lord in prayer. I needed direction for my life.

One day while I was home by myself, Ben turned up. He had a plan. His plan was for me to move in with him. I was reluctant in responding in the positive, but at the same time, living with him would give me some amount of freedom that I longed for. I was no longer in high school; I had no financial support from my parents, so I needed to get a job and be more responsible for my life. Aunt J had done her best, and I did not want to be a burden.

A new day seemed to be dawning in my life. Even though I had not communicated with my mother or father, the fact that I was with Ben, like opium, being with him dulled my pain. Life was good, in my estimation. The nightmares that plagued my life as it related to the death of the twins subsided significantly. Ben was taking care of me. He seemed to be the perfect mate. He would do little things around the house. Neighbours who looked on thought he was a God-sent. In return, I did not ask for much. I had food to eat and a good shelter over my head. I forgot my commitment to the Lord. I hardly prayed or read my Bible, and I stopped going to church completely.

It is so easy to fall into a place of complacency and forgetfulness when life seems to be going well. In my own estimation, life was good, and I was living it. No one was able to talk to me and tell me anything about relationships. I thought I knew what I was doing, but little did I know that there was a master plan for my life, and I could not escape it. The one who watches over me from I was conceived in my mother's womb is in control of my destiny and wrote the details of my life. Even my worst mistakes were engraved in God's plan. The minute happiness I thought I had in a temporary man-made relationship felt like grains of sand in my hands; it just slipped away right before my eyes.

I told myself life was okay, but deep down on the inside, I was sad. I was only lying to myself. One day I was home, my hair was in a mess, and I did not have any money so I made the mistake and told Ben that I needed a hair-do. He looked me squarely in the face and asked, "Mi a hairdresser?" I was shocked to the core of my being. I never asked this man for anything, and the one time I asked him for money, that was his response. I believe that was the day the "straw broke the camel's back." I cried and cried, but I soothed myself with the thought that one day I would get a job. I told him to ask around for any job vacancies, which he did. Ben was well known so he was able to ask.

I saw a radical change in Ben's attitude towards me. He started coming home late at night, and when I asked him what was happening, I knew he was lying to me. He had something to hide but I just could not put my finger on it.

Not long after my inquiries for a job, I was told to write an application letter and resume. To my surprise I was called for an interview and I got the job. Every morning I would travel from Mocho to May Pen. I did not mind. I was working and that gave me some peace of mind.

The year 1996 was shaping up to be a good year, I thought. At home, life changed for the worst. Ben and I had constant disputes; my heart yearned for family. At that time, communication with family was minimal. I had not spoken to my mother, father or siblings in over two years, and I felt lonely. Ben was most times not available for me to talk to. I had no friends, and I felt miserable.

I had no social life. Having a regular job and going to work was the only thing I knew. In the evenings after work, I rushed to get a taxi and head back to the place I called home. Although I was working close to where my mother lived, I never took the time to visit. I was still bitter and unforgiving.

Each day at work, during my lunch break, I would go to the lunchroom which was almost at the back of the building. It was located on the second floor. I would saunter timidly up the stairs and sit at the table next to the window overlooking the main thoroughfare. I was always alone during lunch breaks; I preferred the peace it brought to my mind. Living in a household with six or more persons at any given time was too much of a crowd, filled with clutter and noise, so whenever I got the chance to have a quiet moment it was like heaven to me.

It was a normal day at work and, as usual, I began to walk up the stairs to the lunchroom. However, there was a sound behind me. I turned around to see this gentleman coming up the stairs. I was seeing him for the first time. He asked me shyly, "Can I have lunch with you?" This came as a shock to me; I hesitated for a few seconds, then responded, "Sure." He was my colleague; we worked in the same building, but I never took notice of him. We talked briefly just getting to know each other. Time eluded us; the lunch break of thirty minutes was completed, and it was time to get back to work.

During this particular season of my life, I had no relationship with my mother. We were not communicating, and it hurt me severely. I would pray not just for the Lord to help me get out of the relationship I was in with Ben, but I also prayed earnestly that the relationship between my mother and I would be mended.

As Karl and I began to communicate during my lunch breaks, he became my friend. It was easy for me to tell him about the unstable relationship I was in with Ben. He never offered a solution, and I am glad he did not.

I began to think soberly how to get out of the relationship with Ben without causing a brawl, and I came up with a brilliant plan (so I thought). When Ben got home from work that evening, I decided to start a conversation with him. I told him about my work and the friend, Karl, who I met. Ben asked me pointedly, "Do you like Karl?" I boldly said "Yes." That was the end of the relationship. He began to accuse me of having an affair with someone else, and I did not try to tell him it was not so because I saw this as a grand opportunity to get out of the relationship. That night I did not sleep. We argued for the entire night. I prayed for daybreak. It was the longest night I have ever experienced in history. As day began to break and the sun was slowly mellowing the land, I began packing my bag. I never had any proper luggage carrier, so I put my clothes in plastic bags.

I boarded the bus that morning with approximately four bags in my hand. It was a defining moment in my life; I was finally out of a relationship that bounded me for three unproductive years of my life. I thought I would finally get some peace of mind, but little did I know that I was in for a rude awakening.

It was during the season of lent that I decided to end the relationship with Ben. When I left work the following evening, I went to my mother's house. She was elated to see me, and I was so happy to reconnect with my siblings and my family who I had not spoken to in over a year. As the days and weeks passed by, I spent some time talking with mother. I told her of my ordeal with Ben, some of which I will not mention in this book.

Part Four
A Step In The Right Direction: Journey To Deliverance

"The steps of a good man are ordered by the Lord: and he delighteth in his way. Though he fall, he shall not be utterly cast down..." (Psalm 37:23-24 - KJV).

My Christian walk started at the age of thirteen. Even though my parents were not Christians, they were adamant that I go to church on a Sunday morning, never missing out on Sunday School. Religiously I went to church, not quite understanding why I had to. As I matured, I realized that it was the best thing they could have done for me, besides giving me the privilege of getting a solid foundation in education.

It was a challenge to stay focused on doing the right things all the time. I was living in a social context where Godly living was not first and foremost in the lives of the people I interacted with.

There was no doubt in my mind that I loved the Lord and wanted to truly serve Him.

I was often ridiculed by my siblings and even family members because of my faith. I gave in to the pressure; I stopped attending church and lost all interest in ever wanting to go back. I wanted to be normal. I wanted to eat what everyone else was eating, dress in a worldly fashion, go to parties, and the list went on.

Even though I made the decision to turn away from God initially in a bid to fit in, I never fit in. Everywhere I went I would stick out like a sore thumb. Persons would walk up to me and ask, "Are you a Christian?" Every time I responded by saying "no" there was always an uneasy feeling in the pit of my stomach.

Every time I attended a street meeting or an evangelistic service I was always convicted. I would quickly surrender to the move of the Spirit of God but when I got back home it was a different story. It was easy to fall back into old habits and I did that consistently. I struggled with the conviction of total surrender to the things of God all throughout my teenage years.

I recommitted my life to Christ in the year 1997. This time I was in it for the long haul. It would be remiss of me to tell you that I was always strong. Like the woman at the well who met Jesus, I was searching for things in people and relationships, but these things and people could not fill the insatiable thirst I had. I needed more than what a mere man could offer. As you turn the pages of this book, you will see the many blunders I made.

I fell down many times in my Christian walk, but I was resilient; I refused to stay down. The Lord is always there to pick me up and brush me off. Now I stand resolute, knowing that Jesus Christ, the Author and Finisher of my faith, did it again. Hallelujah!

THE CONVERSION EXPERIENCE

"Come unto me, all ye that labour and are heavy laden and I will give you rest. Take my yoke upon you, and learn of me; for

I am meek and lowly in heart: and ye shall find rest unto your souls." (Matthew 11:28-29 - KJV).

There is a place in God that is beyond human comprehension and understanding. When we yield our stony hearts to the Holy Spirit, the Lord takes us unto Himself regardless of how sinful and wretched we may have been. He takes away our burdens and the weight of sin because Jesus made provisions for us through His shed blood on the cross of Calvary. Our weary soul is then able to find comfort and rest because we are freed from the load we once carried.

It was a cool, quiet evening when Karl came to visit me. We sat outside on the verandah just conversing about the possibilities of life. I was young and impressionable, but I think I knew what I wanted from the get-go. As we talked, I faintly heard the strains of singing. I did not know where the sound was coming from but it drew my attention. There was a church close by; they were having a week of crusade.

Attending church services on a regular basis became a distant memory. I could not remember the last time I went to church. Karl asked me if I was interested in going to see what was happening at church. I was a bit reluctant, but I told him yes. I was clad in a short denim skirt and a burgundy Camisole, so I did not bother to change my clothes. Mother was duly informed that we were taking a walk to the church.

For the first time in years I stepped through the gates of a church. I felt a bit peculiar, but I just did not stop to think about how I was feeling. The church was packed, and people were standing on the outside looking in.

The evangelist was preaching and the crowd was railing. It was like an uproar I had never heard before in my life. Something electrifying and unbelievable was taking place. I saw many mighty miracles; people who were crippled and in wheelchairs began to walk, the dumb began to speak, and deaf ears were being opened. I heard gut-wrenching shrieks and screams coming from people, and it looked like a scene from a movie. I had never seen such manifestations of the power of God. People were falling like flies all over the place. It seemed unbelievable, but deep in my heart I knew it was a great move of God. I became transfixed, watching this man in white shoes reign terror on the kingdom of darkness. Deliverance was evident, and people who were bound and manifesting evil spirits were being freed instantaneously. "What manner of man is this?" was the question that flowed through my mind.

There was a lull in the intensity of the shouts of praise and hallelujahs; people were strewn all over the floor of the church. The preacher began to speak. He gave an instruction for persons who were unsaved and those who needed prayer to make their way to the altar. I was already standing upfront. I did not readily walk to the altar; someone came and whispered in my ears so I stepped forward. The evangelist began to pray and prophesy, and that was it. Men and women began to fall under the power of the anointing, and so did I. It was like an enormous wind began to blow and we had no control over our bodies. Everything changed in a moment.

Those who had the strength to stand went back outside; some went to their seats, while others were still at the altar. We were asked to openly display, by a show of hands, those who were serious about surrendering all to the Lord. My hands went up instantaneously; tears streamed down my face and conviction was in my heart. There was no denying the power of God I saw on display that night. I repeated the sinners' prayer and that was it.

While walking home that night I felt like I was on a magic carpet; I was floating. It was like my legs were not touching the ground. My whole life seemed brand new. I was empty; no weight was on my shoulders. I knew something miraculous took place and it was unexplainable.

I told my mother and sisters about the experience I had and the encounter and transformation that took hold of my heart. The following night, I could not wait to attend church. That particular night, my sister, Tika, surrendered her life to the Lord. It was also the night I experienced the expulsion of evil spirits from my body and the baptism of the "Holy Spirit."

It took less than a day for the transforming power of the Holy Spirit to rearrange my whole life.

The Holy Spirit is real. When you open your heart and believe in the name of Jesus Christ, then the resurrection power is available for the taking. I became a new creation, a brand-new man. All the junk and sins of the past that weighed me down were no longer a part of my life. I could feel the transformation taking place in every fiber of my being. I knew that only the power of God could have manifested in my life and give me a life-changing experience. It was like I was dead, but in a moment, I received life.

The scripture in the book of John, where Jesus spoke to Martha, rings true: "Jesus said unto her, I am the resurrection, and the life: he that believeth in me, though he were dead, yet shall he live." (John 11:25 - KJV). I was dead in trespasses and sins and the iniquities of my past generation were before me. However, Jesus rescued me from death, set me free, and gave me a brand new life in Him. Glory! Hallelujah! My soul had been thirsting for things that could not satisfy, but one night with the King brought a revolution in my life, and everything changed.

I join in harmony with the songwriter who said, "Fill my cup Lord, I lift it up, Lord. Come and quench this thirsting of my soul. Bread from heaven, feed me till I want no more, here's my cup; fill it up and make me whole." The Lord Jesus Christ is and has always been the keeper and the restorer of my soul. The one who filled me with His Spirit and brought wholeness to my life is the true and living God. Without Christ, I can do nothing; I would be a complete failure. But I thank God for the day He rescued me from life's stormy sea.

The days slipped by like I was in a daze. Karl had made a bold step; He surrendered his life to the Lord and that was a game changer. The crusade was over and for some people it seemed that life just went back to being normal, but not for me. There was a fire ignited in my spirit; a constant fire was burning in my soul. I needed more. The Word of God became meat and food. I spent hours reading, trying to understand what I got myself into.

The church was located about five minutes from where I lived so I began visiting the church at 15 Stork Street, May Pen. Every Sunday morning I would get dressed and go to church.

On the 17th of November, two days after my birthday, I was baptized at The Church of the Open Bible at 15 Storks Street, May Pen. Converts class with Reverend Dunk was what I looked forward to on a Sunday morning. Sunday School was where I learnt the basics of Christian living.

As a babe in Christ, I never fully understood the rudiments of Christian living. Karl and I were still dating, and it seemed like it would go on forever. Even though we were baptized and serving the Lord wholeheartedly, we fell back in the pattern of premarital sex. During those moments of self-fulfillment, we came away from the experience feeling guilt-ridden and condemned. We were both living in separate homes and would meet at intervals when we were not working.

Going to Bible study and Sunday morning worship services became my lifestyle, and I really did not desire anything else, only to serve the Lord in spirit and in truth.

What I was not told was that the temptations would come and I must resist, but what about those days when I really did not want to resist? How could I overcome the temptation? How do I live with myself if I give in to the temptation of sex outside of marriage, knowing that I was sinning against the temple of

God? All those thoughts plagued my mind. I was only eighteen years old at that time.

Karl and I began talking about our life and the way forward. I made it clear that I really made up my mind to serve the Lord wholeheartedly. The idea of getting married came to the fore as we discussed the way forward, and Karl decided that it was his intention for us to get married. Before I go any further in writing, I need to point out something to you. Before Karl and I dedicated our lives to serving the Lord, we had some fallouts in the relationship. There were serious issues with trust and speaking the truth. I always had a hunch that he was not always speaking the truth. Nevertheless, I just forgave him for the blunders or mistakes I thought he made and just decided to move forward.

I never saw those blunders as warning signals or stop signs; I just did what I thought was best and continued with the relationship because I never wanted to be the kind of girl who was seemingly unstable, running from one relationship to the next. The truth is, I was having relationships on the rebound although I was blinded to that fact. Starting a new relationship to get over another was not the answer to my problems. This became habitually dangerous.

As you turn the pages and search the chapters of this book, you will come across highlights outlining some dangers of starting a new relationship on the rebound.

Pastor Dunk was duly informed of our intentions to "tie the knot," and so we began premarital counseling promptly. Our parents were brought into the loop in order to give us their blessings. My father flatly disagreed with the idea of me getting married at such a young age. He was also perturbed by the fact that things were happening so fast. My father thought that I did not know Karl well enough to get married. I did appreciate his utterances at that time but looking back over my life now, I recognize that my father saw beyond my need for companionship.

Love was in the air, and I believed it is a pre-requisite for entering marriage. I loved Karl enough to be his bride, and I also believed him when he told me that he loved me, but is love the only basis for marriage? No one could tell me that it was not so. Both Karl and I were working; therefore, we would be able to manage to live life on our own terms and conditions, or so I thought.

As the counseling sessions progressed, the Pastor asked me this question, "Why are you getting married?" I replied promptly, "I love him." I did not realize then that marriage is more than just a fleeting moment of feeling something you cannot explain. If you cannot explain the "why" of marriage, then wait until you can answer before committing.

MARRIAGE

Marriage is a lifetime commitment between a man and a woman to love, honour, respect, and live a life according to God's divine plan. The holy estate of marriage must not be taken lightly and should not be entered in as a means of an escape route from the pressures of life. Everyone entering into a lifelong relationship must first be single and complete. In other words, you will both complement and not just complete each other.

Being complete means that as an individual, you are totally whole and bringing value to the relationship because as an individual you are valuable and able to stand on your own.

Too many people are entering into relationships being incomplete. If you feel incomplete being by yourself, then you are not ready for marriage. This poses a problem for both individuals in the relationship because you will begin to feel like the other partner is unable to completely stand on his or her own. This results in one partner being overly dependent on the other, which allows for an imbalance in the relationship.

True love was all that I desired, and I know that it was the most important ingredient needed to complete the recipe for marriage. As the days drew closer for the ceremony, Karl and I would have disagreements that left me thinking, wondering, "Am I making the right decision? Am I getting married because it is an easy way out of the family house; getting an escape route from my mother once and for all?"

During the time of my conversion, my mother and I would still argue. I just felt like I was at a "breaking point." I was ready to move out of the family home and marrying Karl was a permanent fix to a temporary problem. The instant gratification I thought I would feel was all that kept me going forward with the plans I had for the wedding.

WHEN REALITY HITS

"Anger is one letter away from DANGER." Wherever there is anger, pain is very present.

Time is costly; for every second you spend bitter or mad at the world, is time erased from your life of happiness which you will never regain. Live is too short; therefore, forgive quickly, love unconditionally, and laugh uncontrollably. Regrets are for the weak and faint-hearted; never regret anything that made you smile.

It was youth night at church, the night of the bonfire and a day before our wedding. For some reason there was tension between Karl and me; we got into a very distressful argument. At this point he was adamant about calling off the wedding. I felt disappointed, not sure why the sudden change of heart. I insisted that we move forward with our plans because I was too embarrassed to go back to my parents, family, and friends to tell them the wedding was off.

Prior to this, we had gotten into a few arguments, and during those moments my anger would surge like bolts of lightning hitting a high-tension wire. Karl's eyes widened with shock when he recognized the intensity of my anger. Unknown to me, something was off balance, and I just could not put thoughts together to reason out the "what ifs."

Being preoccupied with all the planning and wanting things to work, I totally ignored the signs around me, especially my anger. At one point, Karl said, "I can't marry you if this is how you are behaving." I was unable to explain to my mother or

70

Karl what was really triggering those bouts of anger. Little did I know that it was a red light, a warning signal to "STOP!" Never use a permanent decision to fix a temporary situation.

LOVED AND LOST

We were both young; he was twenty-one and I was only nineteen years of age. Also, being young in the faith and not understanding how things work both in the natural and spiritual realm prevented me from realizing that something was totally wrong and the Lord was trying to get my undivided attention. I could not hear, neither did I see the tell-tale signs that I was making a huge blunder in my life. I was trying to use a permanent decision to fix a temporary situation. Marriage for me was an escape route to get out of the family house because I just could not see eye to eye with mother. However, I "brainwashed" myself in order to believe the lie that my only reason for getting married was because I had found the love of my life.

Sometimes as young people we believe that we are not easily understood by older folks, or we know more than they do because they are not in our story, but this is not so. The Lord is always watching over us, and He sets persons or destiny helpers on the pathways of our lives. Oftentimes we miss out on the opportunities to make something "wrong" right because we refuse to see the hands outstretched or hear the words of wisdom being uttered from the lips of those we deem to be "church people."

I vaguely remember being pulled aside by a brother in Christ who asked me this question, "Are you sure you want to get married, or do you want to go back to school?" I never had the wisdom at that time to ask him why? My response was "I want to get married." He smiled at me and nodded his head, and that was it. About ten years later, after experience had its perfect work in my life, I saw him. My question to him was, "What did you foresee?" It was only then that he revealed to me what the Lord had placed in his spirit. "Why didn't you tell me?" was my earnest response.

- Never be too quick to answer life's questions in a hurry; give it time and thought, seek counsel, and make the best decision. You can make life-altering decisions on a whim and miss out on God's divine will and purpose for your life.

On February 15, 1997, I made a decision that changed my life and propelled me into a new dimension. Karl and I got married. That particular day the rain fell, and I believe angels cried. We did not have a large ceremony as it was a private wedding comprised of close family and a few friends.

I made myself to believe that life was good. It was a dream come through. I was now on my own, living my life and serving the Lord. I could not ask for anything more.

Karl had a son, and about two months after we were married, he came to spend some time with us. The first night R.J. slept at the house, I sensed there was tension in the room. It was taunt like a tight rope; a sharpened knife would make it impossible to cut. For the first time Karl and I slept "head and tail." I kept asking myself, "What did I do wrong?" Karl seemed upset, and a conversation with him was futile. Sadness gripped and latched on to my heart like a tight glove; I literally felt like a knife was being pushed into my heart a dozen times. I cried the entire night. It was the beginning of sorrows.

Silly arguments became the focal point of the quarrels we would have intermittently. His mother was brought into the picture because he started making complaints to her. I would cook dinner and he would not eat it. He was always making some excuse about the meal not being suitable because that was not how his mother would prepare it.

On a normal workday, I would be home by 5 p.m. One evening I got off working earlier than usual, so I reached home about 2 p.m. As I walked through the gate, I realized something was wrong. As I walked up the driveway, I saw this tall, slim lady walking out of the house. She stood on the outside. When I reached the door, I saw Karl hurriedly taking the sheet off the bed and all he said to me was "I want a divorce."

The young lady was his girlfriend. Karl was still seeing her even when he decided to get married. I was unaware of this because I believed him when he told me initially that he was single and not seeing anyone. Furthermore, he was serving the Lord faithfully. Charm was frightened when she saw me. She began to tell me they were still seeing each other, and He was not telling me the truth. She was the mother of his child and there was nothing I could do about it. I could hardly believe what I was hearing. Was I dreaming? It was actually reality unfolding. It was two months after we both said "I do."

After Charm unveiled her heart, she left the house. I did not know what to do. Karl wanted a divorce; those were his exact words. Like a movie screen, my whole life flashed in front of me. What am I going to tell my family? What will they think of me? Karl was as serious as a judge; the gavel was in his hand, and no verdict was passed, but he decided it was finished. He asked me to go with him to the church and I agreed. As we walked silently to the church, I was numb. I did not know how to respond to the overwhelming situation that was facing me. About two minutes away from the church, I found my voice and I began pleading with Karl, "We can't get divorced," I said hurriedly. "What will people think of us?" Karl listened to my pleas for reconciliation and decided that what I was saying made sense.

Marriage is a serious commitment. This is where two different people with unique personalities devote their lives to spending a lifetime together. It is not something to rush into; proper planning and laying all the cards on the table is always necessary. Notwithstanding, the fact that you put all the necessary things in place for a lifetime of happiness does not mean couples will not go through hard times. They will.

When I look back on those moments of temporary insanity, I wonder why I did not allow him to divorce me then and there. It would have saved me ten years of heartache, pain, and stress, but I remember the scripture that says:

"And we know that all things work together for good to them that love God, to them who are the called according to his purpose." (Romans 8:28 - KJV).

Everything that happened in my life, the bad and the good, the Lord God used it to work out His good plans for my life. Like Jonah, who was sent to Nineveh to warn the people of God's impending judgment, he took a detour and found himself in the belly of a fish. It was there in his "stinking" situation, Jonah cried out to the Lord, and the Lord heard and delivered him. Even Jonah's mistakes were in God's divine plan for his life.

I messed up; I did my own thing in my own way, but out of the rottenness of my situation, like Jonah, I cried out to the Lord and He heard me and delivered me from all my fears. Some persons' deliverance may be instantaneous, while for others, it may take years. Nevertheless, the Lord will deliver you, if you sincerely desire change.

It was early November when I got laid off from my job. Karl had to work a double shift in order for us to maintain a basic standard of living. He told me he was desirous of us having a child because, as he pointed out clearly, we were not really a family until there was a child to call our own. I believed him so not long after I was pregnant with my daughter, Princess T.

I forgave Karl for the lies and the mistakes he made. In my heart I just wanted to live a life pleasing to the Lord and lead a quiet life, one without stress and problems. However, little did I know that I was in for the greatest challenge of my life.

During the process of my pregnancy, I fought many battles, some were physical, and others were spiritual. Through it all, I never gave up on my faith in God. I was resolute in my mind that divorce was not an option, and I would press forward no matter what happened.

The Lord was there with me even in the times when I felt like I was about to lose my unborn baby; the Lord kept me sane. Some of the things I faced I decided not to write because it is too much to even describe. I cannot find the words to pen it. Through it all, I learned to trust in Jesus. I spent most of my days in praise, worship, fasting, and prayer. At other times when I became overwhelmed with situations that I was unable to handle, watching movies became a source of comfort.

Many nights I woke up in fear because I had terrible dreams involving my ex-boyfriend. Sometimes I had dreams of the baby in my womb transforming into demonic spirits.

I never understood much about the spirit realm then, and I did not know what to do concerning the dreams I was having. I consulted with a minister at the church I attended at that time, and he prayed earnestly with me.

Without the earnest prayer of that man of God, there is no telling what could have happened to me or the baby. Some years later, I came to the realization, through prophecy, that someone in my past was determined to do whatever it took to get me back into his life, even if it meant destroying lives.

Be advised, and I must encourage you to take note of your dreams; never take your dreams lightly. Document your dreams if you can. Your dreams are like the pieces of an unsolved puzzle. If you refuse to take note of them, pray and seek help in deciphering the meaning of your dreams, your life can be literally ruined. Dreams are tell-tale signs and symbols of the workings of your life in the spirit realm, which will manifest in the natural realm, whether it is negative or positive. Once it is negative, it must be dealt with from the standpoint of fasting, prayer, and prophetic utterances.

On July 19, 1998, a princess was born. She was and still is an epitome of blessing. Like a candle in the wind, my fears dissipated as I was engrossed and overwhelmed in caring for my baby. There were days when I felt foolish; I did not receive a manual on how to take care of a baby. I prayed and some days I cried, but I did the best I could to ensure that the baby and I were comfortable.

There were days when there was a shortage of food in the house; nothing was in the cupboard to eat, and I had no money. I did not know what to do except pray and ask the Lord to provide. The Lord is true, and His words cannot lie. Elijah was supernaturally sustained as he waited by the brook called Cherith. Even so, I believed that the Lord was able to provide for me. The psalmist pens the scripture that speaks to the experience of which I write:

For he shall deliver the needy when he crieth; the poor also, and him that hath no helper. He shall spare the poor and needy, and shall save the souls of the needy. (Psalm 72:12-13 - KJV).

The Lord is not man, He cannot lie; He is ever faithful, ever true.

Sister Sandra, a wonderful woman of God who lived close by, suddenly showed up at my gate with food to sustain me for a while. Tears welled up in my eyes and "thank you" was not enough to express my sincere gratitude to her for being obedient to the voice of God. This faithful woman of God was there in my life at some odd times. When no one saw or even heard me, she was there listening and stretching her hand to give in whatever way she could.

This woman continued to be a tower of strength in my life, not just spiritually, but emotionally and financially. Most days I did not have to tell her that I was hungry or needed some food to eat. She made it her responsibility to stop at my gate almost every evening when she left work, and there was always something in her hand for me or the baby. There were moments when Sister Sandra, while she was giving me a bag of goodies, had a word of encouragement to lift my spirits. She always had a smile on her face, and if she had a rough day at work I would not know.

Destiny helpers may not always come in the colour, size, or package you expect. What you need to do is to discern who your destiny helpers are, be grateful to them, and pray because they are humans too. They are God's hand and heart outstretched, reaching out to mankind in a world that may seem cruel and unkind.

When you call out to the Lord in your times of need, He will not burst the sky and step down to rescue you, but He will use people who make themselves available to hear Him when He speaks and be obedient when He bids them go.

Since Karl was the only person working and I was home babysitting, it brought a strain on our finances. The landlord gave us notice to leave the house and we had to move. In about one month after we received the notice to move, Karl got another house about two miles or more from where we were living.

Princess T, my daughter, was about three months old at the time when we relocated to our new home. The change in our geographical location seemed to have brought some semblance of unity to our relationship, and Karl seemed to be more at ease.

The new landlord was one of my church sisters. This was good for me because I had someone I could talk to and pray with. Unknown to me, Sister Sandra, my God-given destiny helper, had also relocated and was living less than a minute from my house. I did not realize this until months after settling in.

Less than six months after we relocated, I observed that Karl was coming home late at night. I was not suspicious until one evening, as he walked in, my "spirit man" became agitated and I started praying. The prayers got so intense that I felt like I was at war. Karl seemed shocked at my immediate outburst of prayer and unknown tongue which was erupting like lava spewing from an active volcano. The words coming from my lips were like a flaming sword cutting everything in its path.

A few weeks later, Karl's sister came to visit me. She spoke to me at length about her brother, just wanting to know how we met. I told her everything that I remembered about our relationship. She then asked me, "Is my brother your soul mate?" My reply was off the bat, "Yes." Based on our conversation, Kerry did not believe her brother was speaking the truth. It was only then all my fears about Karl surfaced. Through Kerry's conversation I found out that Karl was still in a relationship with the mother of his child. Every time he had gone to see Charm and came back home to me, my spirit protested because he was playing a dangerous game with his life and mine weighing in the balance. I was in a love triangle and was so blind to it. Karl had little interest in attending church or even praying with me at that point in time. I was shaken in mind, spirit, soul, and body, but I never stopped serving the Lord. Trials taught me how to travail. I learnt how to earnestly pray.

For ten years, I held on to a relationship that seemed to get worst as the months slipped by. There was no respect for self in the relationship. Karl and I, though we professed to be born-again Christians, did not replicate the love of God towards each other.

I tried to fool myself by getting into relationships with persons I thought meant well. I sought comfort from the hands of persons who were only desirous of fulfilling their own selfish needs. I never hid my flaws from Karl; I openly discussed with him the pitfalls I had. The thing is, I wanted to get out of the "fad" of a marriage I was in, so whatever I thought was necessary to get Karl's attention, that I did.

I never really counted the cost of my misdeeds. I just wanted out. I was still actively involved in church. I loved the Lord and wanted to serve Him with all my heart, but I was "handicapped." I felt like a bird flying on one wing. The outbursts with Karl and I were getting worst. I felt trapped.

In the year 2007, the most embarrassing and devastating event took place in my life. Karl and I parted company. The police got involved, and I was sure that death was looming over us. My daughter stood and watched the unfolding of our lives. It was like a horror movie; the only reality was that we were the characters onstage playing the scenes. It was not a fictitious narrative; the event was true to life. For approximately twelve consecutive hours, my body went through a lifeless motion. It was unbelievable.

Karl and I were engaged in a fight, but I will not get into the details of the fight. As I sat in the police station to give the details of the night's event, my mind refused to believe that the scenes that played out were real. It was like I transformed into a different person, and the only question that flooded my mind was, "Is this happening for real?"

I took my daughter, who was about nine years old at that time, with only the clothing I had on my back and went directly to my mother's house after leaving the police station. I had to relive the frightening experience by giving my mother all the details. Everyone was shocked and horrified. My mother became my source of strength and support.

Despite everything that happened, I held fast to the love of God in Christ. There was never a Sunday that I was absent from church. It was hard to focus because church folks who once spoke to me turned their heads away whenever they saw me. I felt like I was in a lonely place, stepping on ticking time bombs.

A few persons who meant me well took me aside and tried to find out what happened. By this time, Karl was making headlines in the church, around the community and on the street. He spoke some things about me that if I did not know myself, I would walk into a moving vehicle.

My only solace was, "this too shall pass" and it did. I was afflicted mentally and emotionally. There were days when I felt so weak and devastated my only safe haven was prayer. When I could not pray, I laid in the bed for hours crying. The Lord heard my cries and He wiped my tears away.

THE TRUTH ABOUT SEPARATION/DIVORCE

Marriage entails the uniting of two souls—they both become one. It is a mystery that only God Himself can explain. On the other hand, divorce is like pulling two pieces of paper apart that were once glued together. When two people, who were once brought together through marriage separate, it literally rips at the soul of both individuals. No matter how terrible a marriage may be, it is oftentimes more satisfying for couples to remain in the relationship than to leave.

A relationship that is dying goes through several emotional phases. No one intentionally gets married to hurt themselves or even their spouse. When a relationship hits rock bottom, each party goes through several emotional stages, whether or not they are the ones who initiated the break-up or not. It is like a tragic roller coaster ride that seems unending. The emotional phases outlined are not in any sequential order as individuals may go through several stages at once or even when they are still in the relationship. I am able to relate to you based on my own experiences. The emotional phases of separation or divorce include:

- Denial - You pretend and speak like all is well when the truth is you are "dying" emotionally.

- Mourning - There is a feeling that something or someone has died, and there is an overwhelming sense of loss. You grieve over the death of a relationship which you planned on, that you thought would have lasted forever.

- Guilt/blame - You will blame yourself for not making better decisions or not working harder to ensure the relationship survived even the worst storm. Sometimes it may be reversed guilt, so you try to make others, like your spouse or other family members or friends, feel guilty for the death of the relationship.

- Bargaining - Damage was done and you feel the need to try to repair and undo the wrong so you may get back together with your spouse.

- Anger - You feel such intense rage, blaming your ex for all your problems.

- Depression - There is no appetite for eating food, changing your clothes, or even taking a shower. All you want to do is stay in bed all day and try to sleep your sorrows away.

- Acceptance - There comes a time when you know you did all that you could and nothing worked; therefore, you feel the need to move forward with your life. Even though the tunnel is dark, there is a light at the end and you are hopeful about seeing that light.

According to Sarah Hall in an online article, there are five emotional stages of separation.

"The 'Five Stages of Grief' was created by Elisabeth Kübler-Ross (1926–2004), a Swiss-American psychiatrist. Her extensive work with the dying led to the book On Death and Dying in 1969. In it, she proposed the now famous Five Stages of Grief as a pattern of adjustment: denial, anger, bargaining, depression, and acceptance. In general, individuals experience most of these stages when faced with their imminent death. The five stages have since been adopted by many as applying to the survivors of a loved one's death or the grieving experienced at the end of a relationship/divorce from a partner."

Hall further pointed out that:

"Having been through the emotional turmoil of divorce myself, I can say that the following stages do not necessarily follow each other in a smooth transition from one to the next (and it can be a bumpy ride!), plus you may find that over the months following a break-up you will experience these stages more than once; the one that matters the most is acceptance as this is where you can begin your healing process."

DENIAL

Denial is your psyches way of protecting you from becoming emotionally overwhelmed. Denial is a useful coping mechanism as long as it does not keep you from progressing on to the next stage. For me, I was at the stage of denial and I was struggling. I painted on my smile and pretended everything was okay in my world. Refusing to face reality is only going to extend your stay in the denial phase and stop you from moving to the next stage.

ANGER

My advice about the anger stage is to LET IT OUT! However, ensure that there are no disloyal ears to hear your rant about your ex, AND DO NOT RANT ON SOCIAL MEDIA; it will come back to bite you on the bum! Seriously, when your world is falling down around you, who better to blame for all your problems than a crazy ex-husband? All the feelings that you hid in the denial stage can now be set free. Anger is probably the one stage that will be repeated over and over until you reach the fifth stage.

BARGAINING

According to Certified Marriage Educator and Divorce Coach, Cathy Meyer:

"Bargaining is a last ditch attempt at coming to terms with the decision to divorce. If you are the leaver, it is during this stage that you will either realize you've made the right decision or a mistake.

If you are at this is the stage where you will begin to pursue your husband/wife. You want them back at all costs to you and your self-esteem. The thing to remember is, they will also go through the Bargaining Stage. If they have made a mistake, they will realize it and undo that which they have set in motion."[8]

Separation or divorce must never be the "means to an end." I consider it a nasty battle that takes a devastating toll on all the parties involved, especially the children. Many times, persons may resort to ending a relationship rather than working it out because of the "hardness of men's hearts." The truth is, there is no winner in the act of separation or divorce. Every individual who decides to end a relationship, in spite of the circumstances, loses something vital and of paramount importance.

---

[8] https://www.beacon.uk.com/author/sarahhall/ Retrieved May 8,2020

BECOMING

Never give up on your dreams because success is not measured by your circumstances but by how you overcome. I overcame many struggles and jumped over countless hurdles as I pushed forward to achieve my goals.

I may have missed the early opportunity to access a good education and career opportunities because I chose to enter into a relationship as a means of seeking a stable life, one I never had as a child. My mother and father, I believe, gave up on me, but God, in His unwavering love, bountiful grace, goodness, and mercy, had His eyes on me continuously.

A door of opportunity opened while I was still married to Karl, and I received a job as a pre-trained teacher in a basic school. The school was owned and operated by the church that I was attending at that time. The money was basically minimum wage but I preferred to work for a little rather than stay home and depend on an unfaithful man. I did not know it was the beginning and the unfolding of a new dimension in my life, one I never perceived.

It was my second time teaching. The first time I taught was in the year 1995 when I just left high school. For a few months I volunteered at the Jamaica Federation for Life Long Learning, formerly JAMAL. I did not like teaching then, neither did I know it was the call of God on my life that propelled me into this field of work because my whole life was centered on having a fulfilling career as a Health Care worker. I love taking care of sick people, so I thought that I would make a good nurse (so I was told).

Even though I went into training as a Practical Nurse, the career I so desperately desired in Health Care never materialized because Mathematics was not my favourite subject, and I needed Mathematics to be accepted at the Kingston School of Nursing. Man can make his plans, but it is God who directs his steps. The Lord was directing my steps through the curves, turns, and disappointments in my life. However, I was blinded, unable to see what God was doing in my life.

I taught at the early childhood institution for one year. The wages I received was minimal and the demand for a better standard of living for Princess T and I was what mattered most. In pursuit of a better life, I applied for another teaching job. At this point I was getting a salary from the school and also a stipend from the Ministry of Education. I was still a pre-trained teacher, therefore, I was not able to receive a full salary.

There was a deep desire to know more about the teaching profession based on this new surge of passion I had developed. Therefore, in 2003 I applied to the Catholic College of Mandeville. The application was accepted, and I was awarded a place in the institution where I began my formal training as a teacher. I worked during the days from Monday to Friday, and in the afternoons I traveled by bus or taxi to Mandeville for part-time teacher training. During this time Karl never made an effort to help me with the payment of school fees. Nevertheless, the Lord saw me through the first semester of college.

Many persons questioned my motives for entering into tertiary education because they thought I was "hanging my hat further than I could reach;" that may have been true then. What they did not know was that I was following after a career that I really did not choose but God, all by Himself, opened a door of opportunity and I was walking through it.

When I did not know what to do as it related to going to teachers' college or pursuing a career in health care, the Lord sent someone to pray for me, and that night it was cemented in my spirit that I was called to teach. It was only then that I stopped fighting the call of God on my life because my dream was to have a successful career as a nurse, but the Lord, who is the author and finisher of my faith, said otherwise.

It was challenging for me to balance work, church, and going to school part-time as a single mother. I struggled sometimes to organize my time, especially with the fact that I had to work overtime to ensure that my daughter was comfortable and there was food on the table.

There were always genuine persons in my life who looked out for my well-being, so the Lord allowed different people to come into my life at various intervals. When there was no money to pay the school fees, I prayed earnestly, and the Lord sent divine help through the hands of humans to bring aid.

During the six years that I took to complete teachers' college, I cannot recall one night that I had to go to bed hungry. Provision was made; Jehovah Jireh, my provider, always sent help in the nick of time.

When I say I am from humble beginnings, I mean there were days when mother did not have food to give my four siblings and I. There were days when all she could find was a little flour which she used to make dumplings. There was no source of protein or vegetable; the only thing that graced the meal of cooked dumplings was melted butter. We ate the dumplings, drank water, and went to bed.

There were times in my life when I thought that being poor was my lot, even though I struggled daily to wrap my mind around the fact that the life I saw my mother living was the life that would be my only reality. Tears became my meat and drink some days. Something within me refused to fully accept a life of poverty. I yearned for more; I craved for a life that was even beyond what I could imagine.

Life was compounded by so many difficult curves and turns that it became extremely difficult to focus on goals, but just to find a way to survive in the moment.

Based on my experiences and the hardships and disappointments I had to maneuver as an individual, I realised that it is easy for young people to give up on their dreams and fall into a lie and the trap of the enemy that "life won't get better." Therefore, it becomes a new normal where the only thing that a teen can do to ease the stress of worrying about tomorrow is to use illegal drugs and engage in illicit sex. This seeks to numb the pain they normally feel daily as they try to rise above ground but keep on failing.

I cannot overemphasize how good the Lord is and has been in my life. I have overcome much through the grace of God. Oh, how He loves me, more than words can say. He loves me more than I can express. No pen can ever write the extraordinary love that the Lord has demonstrated towards me. I am alive and that is everything, even more than money can buy, and the Lord loves you too. Yes, you! Hallelujah. God's love for you is from everlasting to everlasting. There is no end to His Love towards you and me.

Some days when I went to school, I only had enough money to pay my fare and to get back home. Growing up was rough; nevertheless, it never stopped me from dreaming. I wanted a better life, one in which the reality of a meal was not just to eat to survive or to eat just a balanced meal every day, but to be prospering in every area of my life.

Many individuals who knew that I was from humble beginnings thought I was hanging my hat where I could not reach it. The question was asked, "Why would she go to teachers' college when she doesn't have any money?" When you put your trust in the Lord completely, He will send help from the ends of the Earth.

"For I reckon that the sufferings of this present time are not worthy to be compared with the glory which shall be revealed in us." (Romans 8:18 - KJV).

Suffering is for a season; it is working out something good in you and me. There is a glory waiting to manifest, and it can only shine through the pain you have gone through. The glory is coming; wait for it.

In the year 2009, amidst all the struggles I faced and the afflictions I endured during my tenure of study, I graduated from Catholic College of Mandeville with a distinction diploma in Primary Education. It was all God. I could not have done it by myself. If I had followed the trajectory of the words spoken by naysayers, then I would sow to the wind and reap a whirlwind of failures. Thank God that I was persistent and resilient. I was able to bounce back from many slip-ups, dangers, toils, and snares. It's a "BUT God!" that brought me through.

As you read this book, may you find the strength that only God can give to PUSH: Pray Until Something Happens. Never give up on pursuing your God-given dreams no matter the odds that are against you. If God is for you, nothing can stand against you because the Lord is fighting your battles.

PRAYER

ABBA Father, in the name of Jesus Christ of Nazareth and the shed blood of the Lamb, fight against every foe that wars against my God-given destiny. May You lead me and give me the strength to complete that task that seems unreachable. You promise to be with me always. Thank You, Lord, because I know I have the victory in You, in Jesus' name. Amen.

Being confident of this very thing, that he which hath begun a good work in you will perform it until the day of Jesus Christ: (Philippians 1:6 - KJV).

ANSWERING THE CALL

- There is no greater fulfillment in one's life like the overwhelming bounty of joy that envelops your soul when you surrender completely to the Lord. The bitter past that you may have faced becomes a reflection, not a dwelling place. I had to let go of the past hurts and disappointments in order to move forward with hope and see a bright future ahead.

- The past became a source of inspiration and information, which is there to propel one forward. Knowing that God has been good, and He is more than able to keep that which I have committed to Him, which is my whole life, is strength, like no other can give.

- Never allow a fleeting moment of mourning to become a lifetime of loss. Now is the time for women to recognize who we are in the kingdom and not allow the past to inhibit or intimidate our progress.

- God has created humankind with and for a purpose; that purpose is the reason why you live and breathe. As long as you are walking with God, purpose cannot die; you cannot die until you have fulfilled your purpose here on Earth.

- The Lord is able to restore all that you may think you have lost. As long as God is with you, restoration is guaranteed. The Word of God is our constant reminder.

As we read the scripture daily it reminds us and concretize in our spirit what the Lord wants us to know.

Joel 2:25 (KJV) says: *"And I will restore to you the years that the locust hath eaten, the cankerworm, and the caterpiller, and the palmerworm, my great army..."*

The Lord promises restoration to those who have been beaten, abused, rejected, and cast out. Like He did and is doing for the nation of Israel, even so my God will do for you.

PRAYER CHANGES EVERYTHING

Prayer is an authorized system of communion and fellowship with God. Key to the secret place in God, where you are sheltered under the wings of the protector, is the posture of prayer.

He that dwelleth in the secret place of the most High shall abide under the shadow of the Almighty. (Psalm 91:1 - KJV).

Continuous prayer, especially in a particular place, creates an altar that opens a portal to heaven. Jacob had an experience as he went to sleep. In a vision, he saw angels ascending and descending from heaven. This was the place in which his father Abraham built an altar unto God.

"And Jacob went out from Beer-sheba, and went toward Haran. And he lighted upon a certain place, and tarried there all night, because the sun was set; and he took of the stones of that place, and put them for his pillows, and lay down in that

place to sleep. And he dreamed, and behold a ladder set up on the earth, and the top of it reached to heaven: and behold the angels of God ascending and descending on it. And, behold, the Lord stood above it, and said, I am the Lord God of Abraham thy father, and the God of Isaac: the land whereon thou liest, to thee will I give it, and to thy seed;" (Genesis 28:10-13 - KJV).

Prayer is a key that God has given us to open and close doors or gates in the realm of the spirit. It is the believers' way of communicating his or her heart to the Lord. The truth is, prayer was never designed to be a one-way street. When we pray, we must listen for a response. In that way we know that it is an active relationship with our Heavenly Father and not a passive one.

Wherever you are in your walk with the Lord, my brother or sister, ensure that an altar of prayer is established in your life; It is key to your breakthrough and deliverance.

During the early years of my life, a righteous seed was planted as I went to church and Sunday school. I learnt how to pray in my own way. I recognized my need to pray and have a relationship with my Heavenly Father. As I got older, although I strayed from the path of righteousness several times, I never stopped praying. Earnest prayer has been my way of escape from dangers, toils, and snares. Oftentimes I would get anxious when the answers to my prayer did not turn up in the time I expected. I went ahead of myself and tried to solve problems the way I knew how; most times, if not all, situations catapulted me into an unending tailspin of trials. I had no clue how the answers to my prayers would manifest; however, the answers came. In anxious moments of my life when I needed answers, God showed up in His own way and on His own time.

There is always tangible proof that He is always there, waiting for me to surrender my will. This scripture puts it clearly into focus how we should approach the Lord in prayer.

Be careful for nothing; but in every thing by prayer and supplication with thanksgiving let your requests be made known unto God. And the peace of God, which passeth all understanding, shall keep your hearts and minds through Christ Jesus. (Philippians 4:6-7 - KJV).

Not being able to understand the gift of discernment oftentimes caused me to miss out on what God was saying to me in certain seasons of my life. Even though I missed many opportunities to excel both spiritually and academically, the Lord always made a way for me.

The Reverend Apostle N. Ricketts of *Prayer 2000* has penned some powerful points as it relates to prayer:

Please meditate on this short excerpt:

"In the Epistle James 5:16 we read, 'Confess your faults one to another, and pray one for another, that ye may be healed. The effectual fervent prayer of a righteous man availeth much.'

Now, since we are taught to pray one for another and that effectual, fervent prayer avails much, provided it comes from the lips of a righteous man, there must be a reason for prayer.

Why would God make the prayer of faith the condition for receiving? Then what are the reasons for praying?

1. Prayer, from the very beginning, brings us to realize our dependence on God. As the Dead Sea drinks in the River Jordan and becomes no sweeter, and the ocean receives all the rivers and becomes no fresher, so the prayerless man becomes insensible and will not discern God's mercies and kindness.

2. Prayer makes and keeps us humble before God. Having once recognized our dependence on Him and that every good and perfect gift comes from God and "in him we live and move and have our very existence," one cannot but feel humble. Prayer is the act of humility, therefore, humility will cause more prayer, and more prayer will cause more humility.

3. Prayer is one means that creates personal acquaintance and intimacy with God. We may, without prayer, know some things about God. We may believe in God and in His existence and power, but to be personally acquainted with Him means we must become acquainted in the same manner in which we become acquainted with other persons, viz., personal contact, and the only means of personal contact with God is through prayer and conversation with Him.

4. "God heareth not sinners," therefore the supplicant must abandon sin or be defeated in his pursuit. We must be really honest, sincere, and in earnest, we should not live in rebellion against God.

5. Prayer brings man into synchronization with God. Therefore our problems, trials, tests, and heartaches, as well as triumphs, victories, achievements, and conquests belong to the Lord. In turn His problems, interests and concerns, become our passion. In other words, He becomes more interested in us and our affairs, and we become more interested in His.

6. Prayer is the best means through which to assimilate the character of God. To become better acquainted with God, to know God better is to love, admire, adore, and reverence Him more, and while doing so, grow to become more like Him, thus assimilating His very character.

7. Prayer brings us into association with God's perfections. God is the One and the only One to who belongs absolute perfection. Through prayer and closer contact one cannot but be naturally drawn into at least a few of those perfections.

8. Prayer is one of the most effectual means of self-discovery. For example, by talking to God about the imperfections of others instead of to our friends and acquaintances, we may discover that some of those

very same imperfections belong to us in possibly a greater measure than to the other parties.

9. Prayer is the strongest bond of attraction toward God. This accounts for the fact that even ungodly, wicked men almost unconsciously call upon God in times of trouble and serious calamity.

10. Prayer is fellowshipping with God. Fellowship with God brings us into fellowship with His children. Consider the following:

> *"Inasmuch as ye have done it unto one of the least of these my brethren, ye have done it unto me." (Matthew 25:45)*

> *"If thou bring thy gift to the altar, and there remembers that thy brother ought against thee; leave there thy gift before the altar, and go thy way; first be reconciled to thy brother." (Matthew 5:23-24)*

11. Prayer brings us to a greater realization of the hopelessness and perils of the lost. Having learned of, and felt God's love thrilling through our being, we can more readily realize what a soul would miss to lose heaven and our blessed Redeemer, and go to a devil's hell. After days and nights of wrestling with God for lost souls, John Smith buried his face in his hands and sobbed, "I'm a broken-hearted man; I'm a broken-hearted man."

12. Prayer is how we become "labourers together with God."[9]

---

[9] N. Ricketts Prayer 2000

PART FIVE
BEAUTY IN BROKENNESS

Broken people must be mended emotionally, psychologically, and spiritually in order to foster positive, long-lasting relationships.

Being broken is not a reason to end or give up on life, but it is an opportunity to use the negative encounters to propel you into a new dimension, where your experiences bring hope to others, creating a harmonious balance in your life.

The storms of life are tumultuous and harsh; although they may leave you torn and sometimes bitter, they are not meant to bring you harm. As you begin to grow, the experiences you encounter will bend you God-ward.

It does not matter how broken your life may seem, there is always something worthwhile that you can do with the experiences you may encounter. It is often said, "One man's garbage is another man's treasure;" nothing happens by chance; your life is valuable. Here is a story that was told about a "cracked pot" that was seemingly useless:

"An elderly Chinese woman had two large pots, each hung on the ends of a pole which she carried across her neck.

One of the pots had a crack in it, while the other pot was perfect and always delivered a full portion of water.

At the end of the long walks from the stream to the house, the cracked pot arrived only half full.

For a full two years this went on daily, with the woman bringing home only one and a half pots of water.

Of course, the perfect pot was proud of its accomplishments, but the poor cracked pot was ashamed of its own imperfection and miserable that it could only do half of what it had been made to do.

After two years of what it perceived to be bitter failure, it spoke to the woman one day by the stream.

'I am ashamed of myself because this crack in my side causes water to leak out all the way back to your house.'

The old woman smiled, 'Did you notice that there are flowers on your side of the path, but not on the other pot's side? That's because I have always known about your flaw, so I planted flower seeds on your side of the path, and every day while we walk back, you water them.

For two years I have been able to pick these beautiful flowers to decorate the table.

Without you being just the way you are, there would not be this beauty to grace the house.'"

The moral of this story is: no matter your race, creed, or class, all of us as humans may have been broken, hurt, and disappointed by some things or someone at some point in the journey through life. The truth is, the crises you and I faced may have left holes and cracks, otherwise known as flaws, in our personality and even our character, but it is in the times of brokenness that a greater demand is placed on true potential; it allows one to produce something far greater than the mind could ever perceive. Through the broken places of life, one is able to come out better and victorious, an epitome of blessing.

Life as it is has its fair share of trials and tribulations that oftentimes bring you to your knees. As you face life's quest, more often than not, you may not be able to find the resolve to bounce back on your own. It takes something or someone stronger and more powerful than you. Nevertheless, being thrust into a place of brokenness may seem terrible at first, but if you wait, just hold on long enough, you will realize that where you have been broken or knocked to the ground becomes a haven, a source of strength and comfort for others who may have found themselves in similar situations. Furthermore, you can find strength in the Beloved, who will deliver you out of all your troubles, whether great or small.

As I reflect on the broken places of my life, I am no longer bitter; I am getting better daily. The Lord, in His mercy and grace, has given me the strength to overcome. Therefore, as I go through my trials, I am coming out more than a conqueror.

This question has plagued me for the better part of my life, "Why did a loving God allow me to go through such drama in my life and family?" It was not until recently that I fully understood that God will allow you to go through some harsh places. He is the one who chooses your trials and the path you will walk. Why? He knows that He is there with you no matter how hard the circumstances may be.

Like David, the shepherd boy, who spent the better part of his youthful days tending to his father's sheep, and fighting lions and bears just to protect them, the Lord chose him specifically for a task that would deliver Israel from the hands of a tyrant. During that time in his life the Lord was with him. He strengthened and kept him safe. David's brothers were on the battlefield facing Goliath but what David did not know was that his time in the field fighting wild animals was preparing him for a greater victory over a heathen nation for the children of Israel. David, like everyone else, was quite unaware of the task ahead but the Lord knew fully well what is and was to come in David's life and the people of Israel.

Likewise, God has chosen me for an important task. The training I received came from what seemed to be a lifetime of abuse, broken relationships, and some awkward situations. I will explain in further detail how a life of brokenness created a well-spring of healing and deliverance for people who were broken by life's daunting experiences and were made whole by the power of the Holy Spirit working through my life.

No one saw David as King over Israel, but when men look on the outward appearance, God looks at the heart. In the same breath, no one knew that who I am and am becoming was ever possible. I am an ambassador for Christ, His mouthpiece and His hand reaching out to the oppressed, depressed, and rejected.

Part Six
How I Overcame

Once you accept Jesus Christ as your personal Saviour from sin, that is the first step in overcoming the traps and snares of the enemy.

Understanding oneself and the purpose for which life is extended to you as a person is key to living a successful, fulsome, and godly life.

Life is never without its challenges, but when you know your purpose for living, it is the fuel that quickly ignites the lamp on your pathway. No more will you stumble in the dark or wonder hopelessly in the wilderness of life.

You will walk a thousand miles in a day just because you have renewed hope, knowing that the struggles you faced and overcome will be the testimony that saves a life.

Although the Lord allows some things that may be negative to happen in an individual's life, the enemy also sends out his agents after your soul in order to keep you bound in a cycle of negativity, hurt, and disappointments.

Please note that you cannot be too far gone for the blood of Jesus Christ to reach you. When your life is destined for greatness, although Satan may get a glimpse of your future, no devil in hell can stop the plan of God in your life. However, you can be your greatest hindrance to deliverance and breakthrough. When the Holy Spirit knocks on the door of your heart, open to Him and harden not your heart. Your receptiveness to the nudging of the Holy Spirit is key to your breakthroughs. The scripture rightfully said:

Wherefore (as the Holy Ghost saith, To day if ye will hear his voice, Harden not your hearts, as in the provocation, in the day of temptation in the wilderness: (Hebrews 3:7-8 - KJV).

The children of Israel incurred the wrath of God while on their journey through the wilderness. They began to look back from whence they came; they quarreled, murmured, and complained against their Heavenly Father. In order to move forward, you have to seek the things that are Kingdom-oriented, those things that are ahead and not the earthly treasures you left behind in a past relationship.

Brethren, I count not myself to have apprehended: but this one thing I do, forgetting those things which are behind, and reaching forth unto those things which are before, I press toward the mark for the prize of the high calling of God in Christ Jesus. (Philippians 3:13-14 - KJV).

Letting go of past hurts, especially when you have been hurt by friends and family, is like pushing a barrel of water over a hill; it is next to impossible. However, the Word of God, as the compass of life, says that in order for you to get forgiveness from your Heavenly Father, you must first forgive men of their trespasses. The Lord never tells any of us that forgiveness is easy, but it is a requirement that must be adhered to.

Forgiveness is key in overcoming the death traps of the enemy. You first need to forgive yourself and then forgive those who have hurt you. Forgive in such a way that when you see the individuals who harmed you, you will feel godly sorrow for them. It is the kind of forgiveness that drives you to your knees, where you are able to intercede to God on their behalf. I am not telling you that it will be easy, but we have to remember that if we do not forgive others of their trespasses, then the Lord will not hear us when we pray to Him.

"Give us this day our daily bread. And forgive us our debts, as we forgive our debtors." (Matthew 6:11-12 - KJV).

Self-healing is also paramount in overcoming life's traumas. As I began to pray and forgive those who hurt me, I was able to open up and talk about some of the things I went through. The anger and hurt I felt initially began to dissipate, and I began to feel renewed in my body and spirit. The brokenness that was a part of my life was not there anymore. I stopped feeling sorry for myself. I share my experiences with other women and girls who have been scarred through various forms of abuse. In doing this I learnt that there are persons who have experienced far worse trauma than I have and are living full and free lives because of the abundant grace and the healing power of the Spirit of God.

Speak life! The words you utter from your mouth are not just mere words. Creative life is birthed from the spoken word. When you speak positive declarations over your life, they manifest.

Create healthy thoughts. The Word of God states:

"Finally, brethren, whatsoever things are true, whatsoever things are honest, whatsoever things are just, whatsoever things are pure, whatsoever things are lovely, whatsoever

things are of good report; if there be any virtue, and if there be any praise, think on these things." (Philippians 4:8 - KJV).

Be it known that thoughts form words, words form actions, and actions become habits. Whatever you think you become, so think positive thoughts. Meditate on the Word of God. The Word of God is light and life.

"Thy word is a lamp unto my feet, and a light unto my path." (Psalm 119:105 - KJV).

Forget the things that are behind. Those things that are past will grow dim if you allow the Holy Spirit to lead. The weight of sin and the burdens of the past that would want to drive you into a tailspin of fear, anxiety, unforgiveness, and depression, forget them.

Press into God and renew your mind daily through the Word, by singing psalms, hymns and spiritual songs, make melody in your heart unto the Lord. (Ephesians 5:18-19).

Have a support group of prayerful, positive people. Surround yourself with people who love the Lord, have your back, and are able to tell you the truth in love without being judgmental.

Find a quiet place to pray and read the Word. Develop a personal relationship with the Lord. Spend time in His presence so He can talk with you as you talk with Him daily.

Seek professional help. You may pray, read the Word and worship like David, but if you do not get psychological help, you may never pass some hurdles in your adult life. The building blocks of your life will remain stable as you build, if the foundation that you build on is firm. Oftentimes, cracks in our foundation caused by hurts, pain, and disappointments from those whom we love or even strangers, may require a re-inspection and even demolishing the foundation of our lives in order to build a sturdy structure. It takes a level of professionalism and a counselor who has the "know how" to sort through the rubble of our broken lives and help us to start building again.

HOW TO OVERCOME FEAR

Fear is an emotion and also a spirit that can have a negative effect on the human psyche. It can cripple you and leave you motionless both physically and spiritually. It is the absence of love. When you are confident in the love of God, there is no fear because perfect love casts out all fear (see 1 John 4:18). When God created man, man was created in the lower parts of the earth. He breathed in man the breath of life and crowned man with favour; man became a living soul. Fear came about because man refused to listen and completely obey God. Man gave his ear to the devil so the devil sowed the seed of fear in man.

As we sleep, the devil, who is the enemy of our souls, comes and sows seeds of fear and doubt so man not only disobeys but doubts the Word of God.

"But while men slept, his enemy came and sowed tares among the wheat, and went his way." (Matthew 13:25 - KJV).

The antidote for fear is to seek the love of God, which is demonstrated in Christ Jesus.

"For God so loved the world, that he gave his only begotten Son, that whosoever believeth in him should not perish, but have everlasting life." (John 3:16 - KJV).

Furthermore, God, in His great wisdom, never gave us fear, but He gave to His children the spirit of love, power, and soundness of mind.

"For God hath not given us the spirit of fear; but of power, and of love, and of a sound mind." (2 Timothy 1:7 - KJV).

Seek to know the love of God through a committed relationship with Christ. As you read the Word of God and spend time in His presence praying, worshipping, and meditating, the Holy Spirit will bring revelation to your mind, heart, and spirit, so you will know and understand the love of God.

HOW TO OVERCOME LOW SELF-ESTEEM

Self-esteem is the positive projection of oneself based on an individual's view of his or her persona. It is an individual's estimation of his or her own self-worth. Low self-esteem, on the other hand, is a negative outlook or estimation of one's worth based on variables that may be subjected to change. This is a vicious cycle that can plunge an individual into despair and deep depression. This negative cycle can be broken in the following ways:

- Be confident in who God says you are, and do not depend on your own abilities.

  "Trust in the Lord with all thine heart; and lean not unto thine own understanding. In all thy ways acknowledge him, and he shall direct thy paths." (Proverbs 3:5-6 - KJV).

- Do not stress on your own weaknesses; Jesus is the solid rock on whom you stand. Let not your heart be weak, but put your faith and confidence in God and Him alone; He is able to keep your feet from falling and is able to present you faultless to His heavenly Father.

  "Blessed is the man that trusteth in the Lord, and whose hope the Lord is." (Jeremiah 17:7, KJV).

- When you feel your world crumbling and everything is wrong about you, there is great comfort in the Word of God. There is just one you, created in the image and likeness of Almighty God. God purposefully fashioned you; there is no other copy of you. The Lord knew you before you were conceived in your mother's womb; therefore, you cannot be a mistake.

  For thou hast possessed my reins: thou hast covered me in my mother's womb. I will praise thee; for I am fearfully and wonderfully made: marvellous are thy works; and that my soul knoweth right well. (Psalm 139:13-14 - KJV).

Thinking that you are not good enough may be the only and foremost thought that engulfs your world each day. This thought pushes you to feel and seem insignificant in your own eyes. Be encouraged! When David was at the backside of the desert tending to his father's sheep, the Lord God of heaven never saw him as a shepherd boy, but He saw him as King, who would one day rule and reign over His domain and Israel, God's chosen people. David was insignificant in the eyes of his brothers, but God promoted him in their eyes by anointing him to slay Goliath. You can take courage knowing that you are a giant slayer. The Lord is able to take the weak things of the world and elevate you so that you can stand like Mount Zion in the face of those who despitefully use and abuse you.

"But they that wait upon the Lord shall renew their strength; they shall mount up with wings as eagles; they shall run, and not be weary; and they shall walk, and not faint." (Isaiah 40:31 - KJV).

HOW TO OVERCOME REJECTION

Society, church, family, and even friends can leave you feeling like a misfit or an outcast when your life does not match up to their standards or norm, what they think it should be, or when you deviate from their prescribed path and mode of operation. It is very sad because the church must be a place of comfort and stability. Consequently, people run from the church instead of running to it because it is not seen as a safe haven anymore but a place of ridicule, backbiting, and backstabbing. Jesus expects the church to be the church and stand on the commandment to "Love," which is the epicentre of life.

Hannah felt a sense of rejection when she was unable to bear Elkannah a son. Penninah made it worse because instead of praying with her or being a source of comfort, she saw Hannah as competition, infertile and worthless. She teased her so that she wept bitterly. Hannah felt rejected by society, but she found solace in prayer. She communicated to God in her heart, so much so that Eli, the priest, thought she was mad. The priest saw Hannah's affliction and blessed her as she knelt and prayed. The Lord heard Hannah and granted her petition. Samuel was born (see 1 Samuel 1:1-2:21).

Find solace in the fact that God is with you. He hears you when you pray, and He accepts you for who you are because He created you perfect.

"Fear thou not; for I am with thee: be not dismayed; for I am thy God: I will strengthen thee; yea, I will help thee; yea, I will uphold thee with the right hand of my righteousness." (Isaiah 41:10 - KJV).

Again, scripture makes it clear in its exposition of man's rejection. If a mother forgets her child that she nursed at her breast, God will never forget His chosen. It is a great honour to know that the Creator of the universe has you in mind and engraved you in the palm of His hand.

"Can a woman forget her sucking child, that she should not have compassion on the son of her womb? yea, they may forget, yet will I not forget thee." (Isaiah 49:15 - KJV).

Part Seven
Generational Curse

Agenerational curse is a defilement in the bloodline that has passed from one generation to another. You can detect if you are under a curse quite easily. If you observe a consistent negative pattern being replayed in your life, if you struggle with the same bondages that your grandparents, mother, or father, or siblings are faced with, then it is quite possible that you are suffering from the negative effects of a curse.

As I became older, I recognized there were issues in my life that would re-occur on a yearly basis or at certain points in my life. I found it very unusual, and I knew something was wrong. When I spoke to my mother about it, she would often say, "I never knew that my children would come into this world to face the same struggles I went through as a child." That one sentence spoke volumes; it was clear that my mother, at some point in her life, had similar challenges as mine. This led me to ask these questions: "Was it destined for my family to go through such hardships, and why would a loving Heavenly Father allow us to suffer?" These questions plagued my mind constantly until I learned the truth of what was really happening.

There are instances when God commands that a whole family be punished for sin. When we sin whether wilfully or unknowingly it opens a door for our lives to be cursed. The family of Achan sinned and was cursed to death.

"And Achan answered Joshua, and said, Indeed I have sinned against the Lord God of Israel, and thus and thus have I done: When I saw among the spoils a goodly Babylonish garment,

and two hundred shekels of silver, and a wedge of gold of fifty shekels weight, then I coveted them, and took them; and, behold, they are hid in the earth in the midst of my tent, and the silver under it. And Joshua, and all Israel with him, took Achan the son of Zerah, and the silver, and the garment, and the wedge of gold, and his sons, and his daughters, and his oxen, and his asses, and his sheep, and his tent, and all that he had: and they brought them unto the valley of Achor. And Joshua said, Why hast thou troubled us? the Lord shall trouble thee this day. And all Israel stoned him with stones, and burned them with fire, after they had stoned them with stones." (Joshua 7:20-21, 24-25 - KJV).

Be mindful that in some tragedies that you may have faced, you could be ignorant of the root cause as history repeats itself again and again.

When our previous ancestors walked in the way of other gods, and gave themselves over to ancestral worship, idolatry, and witchcraft, it opened a door that would affect an unborn generation. Hence, the effects of our forefather's sin influence generations after generations, if it is not broken through confession, prayer of deliverance, and fasting.

Many young people struggle with things that they were born with, like the nature to commit certain atrocities. It is because it is an act of sin, a transgression that was never repented of, so it is iniquity in the bloodline that made its way to the present generation. The possibilities of a curse being established in the bloodline are noted in scripture according to the book of Exodus:

"Thou shalt not bow down thyself to them, nor serve them: for I the Lord thy God am a jealous God, visiting the iniquity of the fathers upon the children unto the third and fourth generation of them that hate me;" (Exodus 20:5 - KJV).

Here it is being outlined that when the fathers sinned, the consequences of their actions affected generations after them.

Jesus, the Son of the living God, became a curse for you and I, so we can be freed from the curse entrusted on us because our forefathers played the harlot. Therefore, we are not condemned; as individuals, you and I are able to present our case before the throne of grace on behalf of ourselves and future generations. The Word of God expressly states that:

"Christ hath redeemed us from the curse of the law, being made a curse for us: for it is written, Cursed is every one that hangeth on a tree:" (Galatians 3:13 - KJV).

When we should have died without God and a saviour, Jesus Christ redeemed us through His shed blood on the cross of calvary. Therefore, we are no longer walking under a curse, but we are blessed and highly favoured, being heirs of the promise.

The cure for generational curses is repentance. A heart that is turned towards the Lord in confession and true repentance, as well as being sorry for and turning away from evil, will bring true deliverance. When you see this folly, arm yourself with knowledge because there is a way of escape, through Jesus our Lord.

PRAYER FOR BREAKING GENERATIONAL CURSES

Lord Jesus, I confess that You are Lord of my life. You are my Redeemer, Saviour, Deliverer, Master, and Healer. Today I give You and trust You with my life because I know You are able to set me free from the iniquities of my generation. Every past ungodly oath or vow that may have been spoken by my family in past generations that have caused curses to be levied upon my life and the life of my family's bloodline, be broken now and destroyed by the Holy Ghost and fire, in Jesus' name. Amen.

I disannul, in the name of Jesus Christ, and refuse to come into covenant with any form of sin or disobedience that operated in past generations and this present world against the throne of almighty God. I repent for every family member who had given themselves over to sinning against God. I denounce and renounce every sinful act committed in my bloodline, ungodly beliefs, secret societies, and rituals or customs that my family may have participated in or followed willingly or unknowingly. Lord, release me from every curse associated with every anti-Christ spirit and any curse the sins of my forefathers may have produced in and against my life, in Jesus' name. Amen.

LIFE: A SECOND CHANCE

Life can follow a set pattern or cycle. This cycle of life can be one that leads you to make conscious, positive decisions, or you can constantly lean to the negative side where you are always choosing the wrong paths and aligning with people who have similar negative traits.

As was previously mentioned, I was married before and never expected that it would have ended, but it did. For seven years I ran from relationships. There were moments of loneliness, and I would try to get involved, wanting to be loved and comforted, but it was not the right time. I hurt many who showed an interest in me because I was not healed. I had baggage and it posed a major challenge in friendships that blossomed because it caused these beautiful friendships to wither and die. What I never stopped doing was praying earnestly to the Lord, seeking His face, and asking for direction until my husband showed up. God gave me a second chance, and I opened my heart to receive the blessing.

Divorce was never an option for me; however, the circumstances surrounding my life forced me to the edge. The divorce was finalized in 2012 between Karl and me. It left me bruised, battered, and broken in all areas of my life. Nevertheless, God was by my side. There were moments when I was comforted by a song that popped into my spirit or a word of wisdom from my mother. I was never alone; even when I thought I was by myself, the Lord was very present.

In my heart I vowed I would never marry again. I prayed some foolish prayers during the times when I felt hopeless, but I thank God that He is wiser than the earthly wisdom of man. He saw my heart and knew that I was only speaking out of a broken place in my life.

When you are in your broken place, it is easy to speak foolishly out of hurt. I learnt a valuable lesson; never speak out of hurt and anger—you will live to regret it. Sometimes prayer can also come from a place of anger. During those times, I believe the Lord, in His mercy and grace, winks at our ignorance; therefore, we are not consumed.

In 2010, I was still living with my mother. I had walked away from the previous relationship, taking nothing except my daughter, a few changes of clothes, and one pair of shoes on my feet. I was teaching part-time at an evening institute, and that brought some peace of mind. I had a friend who rallied around me and sought to ensure that my daughter and I had sufficient food to eat and clothing to wear. I felt like God was just supplying our daily bread.

Seeking a job with the ministry of education was futile; it seemed the most difficult fete to accomplish as a college graduate who had little experience in the classroom. In order to make two ends meet, I settled for working part-time in private schools. The wages were comparatively thin to what a trained teacher should receive, but it was better than begging.

One day I was home alone and I remember standing under a mango tree at the front of the yard. Loneliness and frustration got the better of me and I burst out in a fit of anger and said, "God, do You mean to tell me there is no good men in Your creation? I need a good man in my life." That day I challenged the Lord but it all came out of frustration. What I learnt later was that the Lord wanted me to be healed so I could be a better person when I entered into a new relationship.

October stepped in bright and cheery. I had forgotten about the rant I had the previous week. I went to work, which was not very far from where I lived at the time. It took me about three minutes or less to walk at a moderate pace to work.

Another school day had ended, and I was just getting ready to go home. As I walked to the office to retrieve my handbag, I realized that there was a visitor in the office. I told the principal he had a visitor and proceeded to take my bag. The gentleman in the white tees and jeans came to the institution to check out some computers that were malfunctioning at that time. Because I was one of the tutors, I resorted to asking Mr. Plummer, the visitor, some questions about the computer. He looked at me and answered my questions in a manner that made me realize that he was quite intelligent and knew a lot about computers. Our short conversation came to an abrupt end but we exchanged numbers for future referencing and I walked home.

During the days that followed, Mr. Plummer and I began talking frequently, like on a daily basis. He was a good conversationalist; I could choose any topic, and he was ready to talk. Due to the fact that I was separated from my previous marriage for three years, I was actually warming up to having a "real friend" in my life. He was living in Kingston, and I was in May Pen. Our friendship grew as we spoke each day; sometimes we had conversations until the wee hours of the morning.

Days turned into weeks, and weeks turned into months. There were days when I felt guilty because I spent more time on the phone talking with this man than I spent in prayer with the Lord. I never recognized that the tug on my heart was the Holy

Spirit calling me to come into fellowship with my Father so that He could direct me. A light literally turned on in my head, "Could this be Mr. Right?" I often wondered if the Lord was showing me a sign that there were good men around.

Sorrow turned into laughter. I was smiling more, talking more, and the burden and weight of my past seemed to lift because I told Mr. Plummer, who became my friend, just about everything. I was never a conversational individual, but all that changed overnight. I eased into the role of a "chatterbox," which was apparently good in my estimation.

One night I had a dream that I saw myself in a picture frame. I was in a sexually immoral act that left me feeling guilty and asking lots of questions in the dream. I never saw the face of the person in the picture frame, only his skin tone. What I did not know was that the very thing that I dreamt was going to take place literally. I was still a child of God, going to church and leading the choir but what I did not realize was that the enemy was setting a trap for me to fall into. I was too blind, too naïve and too caught up to see the enemy at work through the friendship that was being established.

Dreams are like puzzles to your destiny. Sometimes dreams can be spot on and plain like the pictures in a book. There are times when dream symbols are figurative; each symbol represents something tangible in your waking life. Oftentimes the spirit realm is trying to communicate to us using symbolism.

In accordance with my experiences as it relates to dreams, never take your dreams lightly. Knowing the meaning or being able to interpret your dreams successfully may be the difference between you living or dying. I will explore "the realm of dreams" in my next book.

The truth is, I wanted the Lord's approval in order to move forward in a new relationship but I told myself, "This one had to be God." In my soul and mind, I felt like this young man was God-sent because everything felt right. He seemed quite harmless to me. Cunning, intelligent, kind, ambitious, and loving were just a few adjectives I used to describe the persona of Mr. Plummer. On the contrary, he was a backslider who had no intention of recommitting his life to the Lord or returning to the Christian faith. I found out sometime later that he was seeking after knowledge and enlightenment, but God was not in it. That last factor did not seem harmful to me initially as I was mesmerized by the fact that he was a cool guy, not the average young man. He was not interested in material gain, but yet he had the mental capacity to become a prime minister. Prayer has always been my "go to" when I needed direction. I believed that prayer could change even the vilest heathen.

Mr. Plummer was introduced to my prayer partner one day as he stopped by the church to see me. I knew Pat was a prayer warrior; she was not afraid to speak her mind as the Lord reveals His will.

New relationships are formed every day because people on all levels want to have someone who they can talk to and share their innermost thoughts without the fear of being judged.

Hence, human beings are social creatures who are relational, always seeking approval from someone or something outside of themselves.

When individuals are hurting, especially from broken relationships, most times they will seek comfort in the company of family and friends, while others will find solace in isolating themselves from the world around them. As soon as healing has taken effect, one becomes or feels a sense of independence. I believe I was at the place of healing, and I was able to stand on my own two feet after three years living at my mother's house. I had a sense of stability so I decided to get a place of my own. I moved away from mother's house, rented an apartment, and was living comfortably as best as I could.

There were things that I did all in the name of "seeking love and attention." Thank God for grace and mercy that kept me. Thoughts of marriage went through my mind. I really wanted to be committed to one person; that way I would be able to fully lay my life down before the Lord.

Many young persons are of the opinion that they cannot remain single and serve the Lord faithfully. That is a lie. Serving the Lord completely is a life that is fully surrendered to God. The reason young people find it difficult to give all to the Lord is because it demands sacrifice; giving up you. Not many youths are willing to say, "Lord, here I am. Take all of me." Though it is a life of service and sacrifice, it is not impossible. Youths can serve the Lord faithfully.

Discussions of marriage and a devoted spiritual life were the hallmark of many conversations in the two years that Mr. Plummer and I dated. During one of our many conversations, he confessed to me that he did not really want to get married but he would do it only for me. This sparked a biblical discussion around Adam and Eve and his debate was that in the olden days a man would just take a woman and call her his wife.

I became quite uneasy with our relationship because he did not believe in marriage, and he struggled to recommit his life to the Lord. Even though he read the Bible through, it was only to compare it with other literature and to prove a point that Jesus was not necessarily a virgin birth. Suddenly, my antennae went up and we started having numerous squabbles, arguing over simple points that we would normally discuss easily. He also told me he was into meditation and wanted me to try it at some point. The rabbit hole was seemingly getting deeper and darker, and I was a bit fearful of where it would take me.

One day I woke up with many questions about where our lives were headed and he was unable to supply me with the answers. The possibility was that Mr. Right seemed "wrong," and the only thing I knew how to do was to pray.

In the days following, there were some discoveries I garnered about Mr. Plummer. I made a conscious decision to go on twenty-one days fast. The purpose of the fast was to seek God's will and direction in the matter concerning me and Mr.

Plummer. I wanted answers such as what religion he was into and if we were meant to live "happily ever after."

Earnest prayer and seeking the face of the Lord was my daily routine as I locked myself in my room for twenty-one days. At the end of the fast, I called Mr. Plummer because I felt the need to talk to him face to face. He responded to my invitation to speak to him so the time was set. The Lord did not speak to me directly during the twenty-one days that I fasted and prayed, but something unusual happened. As we conversed, I began asking him some questions. At the moment that I was asking the questions, the Lord revealed to me that he was in some kind of "New Age Movement." He was completely shocked and asked me how I knew. I told him the Lord revealed it to me. From that point onwards, there was a divide in our communication; our conversations became less, and I began to feel sad and depressed. I prayed and asked the Lord to deliver me from that relationship. He was paying my rent at that time because I did not have a steady job. I never knew that when I prayed and asked for direction, the Lord heard.

Day and night are certain; as the sun sets each evening and rises in the morning, so is God's love for me. Sure! After a couple of months, a friend of mine and ministry partner got a place for me to live. Mr. Plummer had moved from Kingston and occupied two rooms of the house that I had rented previously.

The Lord took me out of a place of depression and sadness, even though the house was comfortable, and put me in another place that required of me to live on my knees, being in prayer daily. That place was volcanic, like a hot lava battleground.

Witchcraft and evil were at its highest peak in that place; only the spiritually fit and fortified could survive. It was a rescue mission for another dear friend and sister and also the springboard that catapulted me into my God-given destiny. However, little did I know that the devil had another plan designed to kill me, but God! My God rescued me and gave me another chance. It was in this "move" that God revealed the "man of my dreams," my husband, ministry partner, lover, and friend.

Part Eight
Transformed By Grace

"The hand of the Lord was upon me, and carried me out in the spirit of the Lord, and set me down in the midst of the valley which was full of bones, and caused me to pass by them round about: and, behold, there were very many in the open valley; and, lo, they were very dry. And he said unto me, Son of man, can these bones live? And I answered, O Lord God, thou knowest. Again he said unto me, Prophesy upon these bones, and say unto them, O ye dry bones, hear the word of the Lord. Thus saith the Lord God unto these bones; Behold, I will cause breath to enter into you, and ye shall live: and I will lay sinews upon you, and will bring up flesh upon you, and cover you with skin, and put breath in you, and ye shall live; and ye shall know that I am the Lord." (Ezekiel 37:1-6 - KJV).

As I pen the multiple episodes of my life, I reflected on the many roads that I traveled and the kaleidoscope of experiences that adorned, etched, and painted the landscape of my existence here on Earth. Hopelessness, disappointments, separation, and loss were like old rags that draped my slumped shoulders; with head hanging low, and dark, sunken sad eyes that seemed to pierce the ground below, my feet dragged my listless body as I tossed to and fro like a broken limb in the raging wind of defeat. My life was like a valley of dry bones; beaten, bruised, and feeling defeated and hopeless.

The sovereign Lord looked down on Earth and saw me in a valley of dry bones. He spoke to this prophet, and the question was asked, "Can My daughter live?" No matter how hopeless your life may seem or have been, there is a God in heaven who is able to render every evil in your life null and void. He is able to resurrect that which seems to be dead and decaying just by speaking one word into your spirit. The Word of God spoken to man is quick and powerful, sharper than any double-edged sword (see Hebrews 4:12). When the Lord speaks, things must change.

Prophecy or the spoken word from a prophet called of God is necessary in the life of any individual who is seeking godly direction and order in his or her sojourn here on Earth. Prophecy reveals the heart of God to mankind.

This charge I commit unto thee, son Timothy, according to the prophecies which went before on thee, that thou by them mightest war a good warfare; (1 Timothy 1:18 - KJV).

This scripture highlighted Paul's words to Timothy, charging him to hold fast to the prophecies that were spoken over him because those words which were spoken were life-giving and would help him along his journey. The gift of personal prophecy is very important to the life of a believer. Notwithstanding, there are many flaky and false prophecies that have gone up over people's lives that wreaked havoc and even destroyed many lives. This is not reason enough for you and me to despise personal prophecies. The vast expanse of true prophetic voices spanning the Old and New Testament era is conclusive evidence that true prophecy is key to locking and unlocking many doors, winning battles, and bringing mighty men of valor into great victories, and kings to their knees.

The prophetic voice of great men and women, who came into my life at various intervals, was the voice of God that directed my life and set me on a new pathway that reflected growth and transformation. This came only through the unmerited favour of God's grace.

As I continually seek the Lord to unravel His blueprint for my life and bring me into alignment to fulfill His divine purpose, the personal prophecies I received were like roadmaps that charted and illuminated my pathway. Without true prophecy, my life would be a wreck. I thank God for all those great men and women who, as they were inspired by Holy Spirit, spoke as oracles over my life at a time when I needed Godly direction.

SPIRITUAL WARFARE

Spiritual warfare was not new to me, but the level of warfare I had to fight in my new home was at an all-time high. Even though it required much dedication to prayer and fasting, I was undaunted and fearless. I knew first and foremost that my battles were not physical, neither were they with man, although humans allow themselves to be used as demonic guest houses and agents of the dark realm. I kept reminding myself that I wage war, not against the flesh but against principalities and powers

"For we wrestle not against flesh and blood, but against principalities, against powers, against the rulers of the darkness of this world, against spiritual wickedness in high places." (Ephesians 6:12 - KJV).

Every level of warfare you encounter and overcome prepares you to step up in rank for the next level of warfare. As believers we are in a constant battle; we wage war even with our own self. Paul makes mention of this in his epistle:

"For the flesh lusteth against the Spirit, and the Spirit against the flesh: and these are contrary the one to the other: so that ye cannot do the things that ye would." (Galatians 5:17 - KJV).

There is a constant war in our members; therefore, you will find yourself doing things you do not really want to do because you know it is wrong. The struggle is real.

"For I know that in me (that is, in my flesh,) dwelleth no good thing: for to will is present with me; but how to perform that which is good I find not. For the good that I would I do not: but the evil which I would not, that I do." (Romans 7:18-19 - KJV).

No matter how spiritual we are, we get caught up in the things that are contrary to the spirit. That is why self must be placed on the altar daily so that only the beauty of Jesus will emanate from our members.

During my tenure living at Paisley Avenue in May Pen, the Lord blessed me with a wonderful housemate, friend, and sister. Cher and I share similar personality traits, which caused our friendship to blossom, especially when she realized that I had her back.

My friend was the principal of a prominent private preparatory school in the same vicinity where we lived. She knew I was unemployed so she hired me to teach the grade six class, which was sitting the Grade Six Achievement Test the following year. It was a divine setup that could only be orchestrated by God. Not only was I living in a house free of cost, but I was also offered a teaching job without doing an interview; I did not even apply for the job. That is favour!

When you make up your mind to really serve the Lord, He will not withhold anything good from you. The Lord Himself will make streams in the desert and a highway through the mountain for you to cross over, just so that you can be at peace.

Every episode, blunder, mistake, and strategic point in my life, reverberates the very tangible presence of God. I never saw or felt it then, but I see it now as I write. Hallelujah! He was there working behind the scenes of my life, even when I thought I was alone. Glory to God! He is an awesome wonder! How great! How great is my God!

For every season of my life there are lessons to learn. I did not know then that even the hard places, the thorns, embarrassment, and disappointments were actually keys that would unlock the hidden potential that was within. I murmured, complained, and even became bitter with God. When things got rough, I felt like I was in a wilderness all by myself, climbing the harsh, rugged terrain of a mountain, and my only hope of ever surviving was to continue climbing.

"Abandonment" or, for want of a better word, "rejection" was like a halo around my head. I felt abandoned by family and some who were supposed to be my friends. Not realizing that I hid myself from the eyes of the world, I was in and out of

136

depression, and the place I laid my head did not bring any comfort to my troubled mind. I felt like I was in a pit. I had left my daughter with a friend who was like a sister to me. Debbie took care of my little princess like she was her own daughter. This brought some relief to my mind. I knew that Princess T was okay.

Day and night my tears became my meat and drink. I missed my daughter; it was actually her first time being separated from me for a long period of time. She was just in ninth grade in high school, but based on the level of warfare I was fighting and the physical condition in which I was living, I could not allow her to be in the same space with me.

Fasting, prayer, worship, and the Word were what kept me sane; there were times when I felt like I was going out of my mind. I was sharing space with Cher, who was undergoing tumultuous warfare so there were days when I had to forget about myself and intercede for my dear sister. During that season of my life, the Lord revolutionized my prayer life. The materialistic person I had become began to lose interest in material gain. It was never easy to lose to self, but in order for me to get to where God intended for me, I had to learn the lessons quickly.

WITCHCRAFT

From the moment I moved in with my friend Cher, I got an impression in my spirit that I should not eat from or trust anyone at the school. The property on which I lived then comprised of a house and a school with a tuck shop and a canteen.

There were days when I was at school and had no lunch or money to purchase a snack. I could not eat anything that was prepared. For days, I would just go over to the house, pray, and get back to class. Teaching in that particular institution was a constant battle. The physical environment had the appearance of being calm and friendly, but as I engaged in prayer, it was a constant battlefield.

One morning I went into my classroom earlier than usual and on my desk and chalkboard I could see the impression of something oily. Underneath my desk was covered with white powder. I thought I was in a dream. I was so angry in my spirit that I felt like my breath stopped for a few seconds.

I knew then that I was up against human agents assigned by the devil. After that incident, for days and weeks I felt like someone was watching me. Every time I would turn to the left, a strange feeling would come over me. Fear was not a part of my vocabulary, so I intensified my prayer life by fasting and praying at regular intervals.

There was a need to incorporate prayer into the school so I made it my point of duty to meet with the teachers at least once per week to pray during the first break in the morning. I observed that during our morning prayers at school, some teachers became quite nervous, and I prayed even more.

Someone who was a part of the school family was not comfortable with what I was doing in terms of praying because the Lord was revealing secrets that they did not want to be in the open. There were days when I was feeling sick, heavy like lead, but it never stopped me from persevering in prayer because I was determined to help my sister Cher to stand on her feet again.

As I mentioned in a previous chapter, humans can give themselves over as agents to carry out the works of evil for the kingdom of darkness. Even though we wrestle not against flesh and blood, humans will give themselves over to be used as demonic portals for the dark realm.

There was much demonic, witchcraft activities taking place on the property where I lived. It had to take God Himself to keep Cher and I from the horrors of death and doom. Every week there were powerful prayer meetings. Youths from various churches would meet on the verandah, worshipping and praying. This medium of pouring out to the Lord was also a place of strength after each battle that was encountered.

There were nights when sleep evaded my eyes and I had to be praying, storming heaven for God to release angels to do battle on behalf of the owner of the house and school property.

Some people may say witchcraft is a fad or a figment of one's imagination, but I must say that an unbeliever is more in danger of falling into the traps of this wicked scheme. Witchcraft is real and must not be taken lightly. There are no powers greater than the power that raised Christ from the dead. However, just as how the Spirit of the Lord moves upon man and extraordinary manifestations take place, it is similar with the dark realm. Be prayerful; be wise.

Be sober, be vigilant; because your adversary the devil, as a roaring lion, walketh about, seeking whom he may devour: Whom resist steadfast in the faith, knowing that the same afflictions are accomplished in your brethren that are in the world. But the God of all grace, who hath called us unto his eternal glory by Christ Jesus, after that ye have suffered a while, make you perfect, stablish, strengthen, settle you. (1 Peter 5:8-10 - KJV).

When you are ignorant of the devices of the devil, that is when you are most vulnerable to fall into his traps.

Faith eluded me on many occasions; there were days when I wavered in my faith. Hope for a better tomorrow was nowhere in sight, but I never lost sight of why the Lord took me to the place I was living. What I did not realize was that my life was being transformed even as I was praying for someone else's breakthrough and deliverance. Even though my life, as I had envisioned, was nowhere near what I had in mind for a future, I placed it on the altar of prayer and sacrifice.

THE LORD HONOURS SACRIFICE

"He that loveth his life shall lose it; and he that hateth his life in this world shall keep it unto life eternal. If any man serve me, let him follow me; and where I am, there shall also my

*servant be: if any man serve me, him will my Father honour."
(John 12:25-26 - KJV).*

As I lay aside my ambitions, my plans, and my way of doing things, the Lord gained access to the throne of my life. It was only then that He was able to establish His will in my life. Glory! Today, as you read, make Jesus the centre of your world by laying down your life so He can lift you up in honour.

DIVINE SET UP

The leader of the prayer group of which I was a part decided to take a few members to a youth summit in Barbados. During the time that I was a part of this prayer group, Damian*[10] (the leader) and I were dating. It was prophesied that we were to be husband and wife so we both leaned towards the prophetic, always praying on the matter. It did not always rest comfortably in my spirit that it was to be so; therefore, I kept praying, asking the Lord to reveal what I could not see or hear.

In July 2013, amidst all the struggles of getting the airfare for the trip to Barbados, Damian and Okino persevered, and they came up with the money; the Lord provided. Only three members of the youth group were able to take the trip to Barbados, Damian, Okino, and myself, who was the only female. It was rather disappointing that other members of the youth group were unable to attend the conference so we saw it as a privilege that God in His infinite wisdom made it possible for us to attend. We had no clue what was about to happen.

---

[10] *Not his real name.

Traveling for the first time to Barbados was most eventful, memorable, and life-changing. We stopped over in Trinidad for a short while because it was a connecting flight. The hours flew by quickly and it felt like a moment's breath. There was a buzz of excitement in the air; I was not sure what it was about. My heart was abuzz with worship and praise to the Lord. I did not have any spending money, neither was I responsible for purchasing the tickets, all I knew was that I was on a plane to a powerful and life-changing conference "Eagles Eye."

The moment the plane landed in Barbados, everything changed. Ministry began to take effect the moment our feet touched the ground. Seeking the face of God in prayer and fasting during our meetings prior to the trip to Barbados was like opening a portal over our lives for the prophetic voice to come alive.

Ministers at the conference just prophesied over our lives as I have never seen it before. In one of the prophecies, it was foretold that there would be a marriage in the youth group. It left me a bit puzzled because Damian and I, though we were dating, were not ready for marriage. I tried to push it out of my mind, but it seemed futile.

Prior to the prophetic utterances, Okino and I were sitting at the breakfast table; I believe it was the second day of the conference, and for some reason I felt an impression in my spirit that he was thinking about me. I beckoned to him across the table, and he stepped outside. I followed him on the outside and pointedly asked him this question, "Are you thinking about me as someone you want to date or to be your wife?" I could feel a strong tug on my emotions, but Okino never looked at me directly. He just looked down at his feet and smiled. Inwardly, I knew what the answer was; it was confirmed in my spirit without him saying a word. Damian and I literally felt like strangers in Barbados. I was not sure what was happening, but I literally felt like we were being torn apart.

For the first couple days in Barbados, I felt emotionally unstable. I was unable to interact or connect with Damian because we were not housed in the same building, and when we met for gatherings, we had to interact with other youths. This was rather strange to me because while we were in Jamaica he was always by my side, no matter the circumstances surrounding us. Damian was also a tower of strength in the times when I needed it most. He would pray me through some of the most difficult times during my stay at Cher.

I needed to talk to someone; I just could not understand the void that stood between Damian and I. Camp counselors were available at the conference. I found a camp counselor who was also one of the presenters. I needed answers quickly. "Why was I feeling so unattached to Damian?" On the contrary, I was missing him terribly. The camp counselor spoke to me at length and advised me on how to proceed. In my heart I knew that the relationship between Damian and I had to end; I didn't want to accept it then.

God has a way of shifting us into alignment with His will and purpose for our lives. Even when we do not see the pieces of the jig-saw puzzle fitting together, the Lord knows the beginning from the end and orders our steps in tandem with His will. Traveling from Jamaica to Barbados not only caused me to shift spiritually but physically and emotionally as well. The months that followed were proof to show me that God was in control of my life, and He chooses whomsoever He wills.

While I was worried about the fact that Damian and I were at odd ends, Okino was there for me. I spoke to him about what was happening to me and all the time talking, I tried to hide the tears that were burning to be released from my eyes. Okino did not say much, he just listened to all I had to say.

Kevin was the gentleman who hosted Okino during the length of the trip. He was very kind and offered to take me out for lunch. Kevin had to go back to his house to take a shower before lunch. This took the sting off me waiting on Damian to show up; he never did. While I waited at Kevin's house, he went into prayer. In the midst of praying, he began to prophesy to Okino and I saying, "Before the year is out, December, you will be together." Those were his words to us. Our mouths opened in shock. I did not understand how that was possible, but if the Lord said it, it was so. After lunch with Kevin and Okino, we went shopping. My mind was buzzing with the word; questions were popping in my head, and I did not have the answers.

After about two weeks of ministry in Barbados, it was time for us to return to Jamaica. Without a shadow of doubt, I knew that something supernatural took place in Barbados, and I was certain that my life would never be the same again.

When I got home, I felt like my time was coming to a close as it related to where I was living. To make matters worse, Damian and I were not seeing eye to eye. God was up to something, but I was unable to see the signs pointing me in His direction.

It was a gloomy day. The grey clouds hanging overhead seemed to reflect my innermost feelings. As I lay on the bed with my eyes closed, I was reflecting, meditating, and thinking about my life when suddenly, like the blast of a bullet from a gun, I heard the loudest "NO" resounding in my head. It was the loudest no I had ever heard in my entire life. My eyes flew open, and I jumped off the bed. I rushed into the restroom and uncontrollable tears like a river flooded my face. I knew exactly what that no meant, and it broke me to pieces.

How was I to tell Damian that I was praying about our relationship and the Lord said "No"? I knew the Lord spoke, and I could not ignore it. With tears in my eyes, I told Damian what the Lord said to me. It was like a slap in my face; it was like a horror movie coming to life.

Days and nights of continuous arguments unleashed a deluge of pain upon my person. I was made to feel like the worst possible criminal because I decided to end a relationship that the Lord did not agree with. Comfort and peace came to my spirit when the Lord reminded me through His Word that it is better to obey God rather than man. I became an enemy to many who I used to talk to, counsel, and pray with me, but again, prayer became my hiding place.

Through the storms of insults, accusations, and shame, the Lord was working something far greater than I could ever possibly imagine. There were days when guilt rocked my world; how could I have fallen prey to another trap of the enemy after what seemed like a continuum of failed relationships, a life streamlined with mistakes and regrets.

How did I find myself in such a mess? My heart was broken in a thousand pieces again and again, but I thank God for some friends and prayer partners who never relented; they stood by me day and night, praying me through days and nights of an endless word storm. The blows were vicious, hitting below the belt and even the core of my soul.

There were days when I felt tired, sorry for myself, and I wanted to die. I never envisioned my life to be a constant battlefield. Strength was garnered from renewing my mind daily through the Word of God. Struggles will come and disappointments will surface when you think it not, but the Word of God, which is true, sharp, and powerful, is able to correct, heal, deliver and set you free.

Like a diamond in the rough and gold tried in a fiery furnace, the afflictions in my life were there to purge, purify, cut off, and bend my life God-ward.

"Many are the afflictions of the righteous: but the Lord delivereth him out of them all." (Psalm 34:19 - KJV).

The word of God spoken from the mouth of a prophet is likened to a compass that is able to lead you where the hand of

God can reach you. As it was prophesied over my life in Barbados, it manifested five months later.

In December 2014, the heavens opened over my life, and it was revealed to Okino and I in a most unique and unforgettable way that it was the Lord's will for us to be husband and wife. Okino came to visit me one evening at home. Cher, Dian, and myself were sitting on the front porch conversing. The morning of the same day I was in prayer and the Lord gave me a song. It was impressed upon my heart to share the song with Okino, but I did not tell him. As he walked in, I informed him that I had a specific song for him to listen. He then told me that he had a song to share with me as well.

Okino then proceeded to play the song that was laid on his heart. I listened quietly, but even as I listened to the lyrics of the song, I could feel the words piercing my spirit like sharp arrows and tears filled my eyes. At the end of the song, I then scrolled to the playlist on my phone and touched play. The melody and the lyrics of the song penetrated the atmosphere around us with an electrifying resonance. Shock reflected from our faces like lightning. The words of the songs were answers that we sought.

The ways of the Lord are a mystery; man can never search out the thoughts of God because man is so limited in his finite understanding of an infinite God. We put God in a box and say, "that's God," but on that super special day when the heavens opened over our lives, we recognized the vastness of the thoughts of our Heavenly Father towards humanity.

Dating was the farthest thing from our minds. Okino and I never dated; we did not even get the chance to really know each other. It took three months, with the help of Holy Spirit, Dian, Cherine, and some other persons who the Lord allowed to be in our lives at that point in time to plan the most beautiful wedding ceremony ever.

Port Royal was our destined place to exchange our vows. March 30, 2014 was a major turning point in the lives of Okino and I. Approximately eighteen persons journeyed to Foreshore Road. The beauty and brightness of the morning glow that hovered above the waters was a replication of God's glory resting upon two individuals who decided to allow the Spirit of the Lord to pave their way forward and unite their hearts in holy matrimony.

Joy flooded our souls and bubbled forth from our lips in fits of uncontrollable laughter. Prayers ascended under the open canopy of the heavens as we stood on the shores of the Caribbean Sea; tears of joy wet our faces as Holy Spirit kissed us with His tangible presence. The most memorable and unforgettable moment in our lives was witnessed by passersby, families, well-wishers, ministers, and most of all, the Almighty God, and Holy Spirit.

PART NINE
CALLED TO MINISTRY

A new season in both our lives began to unfold. Everything was new. Nothing we had heard or seen was enough to prepare us for the life and the ministry that was entrusted to us immediately.

In the eighth month of the wonderful union between Okino and me, an invitation was extended to us. We were told there was a church in Manchester that needed a pastor. Being enthused and zealous for the Lord and ministry we decided to pray about it. Prior to us getting the invitation, during prayer, a dear minister and sister in Christ prophesied that an engagement was about to manifest as ministry for us. So, one Sunday morning, after much praying and seeking the Lord for direction, we visited the church. It was a small church with less than five visiting friends, one member, and the pastor.

The church was in Manchester, and we were living in May Pen. Every Sunday morning we chartered a bus and traveled to Spaldings, Manchester for church service. On many occasions, when we entered the church on a Sunday morning only one person was there along with the pastor. We knew we had work to do.

Okino accepted the offer to assist the pastor at the church with ministry. We met Sunday after Sunday at church, just praying at the altar and seeking the Lord for direction. The church door was open, but the pews were empty. Dian and Cherine were like armour bearers; they prayed for us in that season of our lives, and the Lord was and has been faithful to answer prayers that were prayed earnestly from sincere hearts.

"The effectual fervent prayer of a righteous man availeth much." (James 5:16 - KJV).

When consistent prayers are being prayed from the hearts of men and women who seek to live a daily consecrated life, the Lord hears and answers.

The youth ministry began growing a few months after we began assisting with the work at the church. On Friday nights there was an outpouring of over sixty or more youths from the community and surrounding churches. The move of the Holy Spirit was evident in our midst and the lives of people within the community began to change. All glory, honour, and praise to Almighty God, who is the keeper of men's souls.

It was tiresome to travel from May Pen to Manchester every Sunday and sometimes twice per week for ministry, but we never complained. It was all in a bid to see the work of the Lord and the kingdom of heaven manifest in the lives of people who yielded themselves to the Spirit of Almighty God.

After one year of ministry in Spaldings, with the recommendation of the pastor and testimonies from other ministers, Okino and I received our ordination as pastor and minister of the gospel of Jesus Christ.

God did it all by Himself. He turned my life around and transformed me into the image of His dear Son, Jesus Christ. Over and over, He moulds me and makes me. Into His own likeness Jesus fashioned the broken lump of clay, and made me into another vessel.

EMPLOYMENT

The Lord opened doors of opportunity for me that no man can close. After months of praying and seeking the Lord for a job, I was called one week before school reopened in September of 2014. The principal of the school where I am presently working asked me if I could show up for work the Monday morning. I had no previous interviews; all I knew was that I was asked by my friend, Cher, to apply to the school for a position as a classroom teacher.

Employment was immediate and final. It was a permanent fix; my Heavenly father did it for me. In less than a year of marriage, I was employed, strategically hand-picked for a position that I was not even interviewed for, called to pastor a church for which I knew nothing about, and ordained as a minister of the gospel of Jesus Christ.

Promotion comes not from the east or the west, but from the Creator of heaven and earth (see Psalm 75:6). Hallelujah!

No one can ever understand how the Lord took me from nothing and made something beautiful of my life, not that He is through with me. I am a "work in progress." The Lord can do the same for you; with or without a masters or a degree, the Lord is able to elevate you and position you in places you never dreamed of.

No matter how messed up your life may be, if you give it back to the Lord, He is able to fix the broken pieces of your life and use you to be a blessing to others.

Never be ashamed of your past when the Lord lifts you from the pit of despair because whatever you go through, there is a level of grace that you receive to help pull others out of their situation. I know this to be true because of how the Lord used me and is still using me to help women who have been abused to be completely delivered and set free from the bondage of fear and shame.

After the ordination in October 2015, doors began opening for ministry on other platforms. On one occasion I was asked to minister at a Women's Retreat in Ocho Rios. It was my first time engaging in ministry of such a large proportion. As I spent days in prayer seeking the Lord for a word, it was impressed upon my heart that I needed to share my life's experiences while laying a foundation with scriptures.

I was obedient to the Spirit of the Lord and spoke about my life in detail. I could hear the sound of weeping and shouts of hallelujah during intervals but, for the most part, these ladies remained quiet. After delivering the word that was laid on my heart, I proceeded to ask persons who had been hurt and needed prayer to make a queue; to my amazement almost all the ladies stood. For almost two hours the Holy Spirit gave me prophetic utterances to minister to the hearts of over thirty ladies who were rejected, broken, bruised, battered, and some left for dead.

The anointing that flowed over me that night came from a place where I was also broken at various points in my life, but through the power of the Holy Spirit, I am healed, delivered, and set free. With a heart of love and compassion for the lives that stood before me, the Lord entrusted me with the power of His Spirit to impart wisdom, knowledge, deliverance, and healing to those who needed it most.

When you are faced with a difficult past, take it to the Lord in prayer. He is more than able to take away the pain and erase the stain of sin. He did it for me, and He can do it for you too.

Refuse to die in the wilderness situation that you are facing. The uncultivated, uninhabitable, or inhospitable places in your life are a representation of the desert you are going through. It is a position that is unfavorable with the wonderful dreams that you may have for your life and also the master blueprint that your Heavenly Father has to restore, rearrange, and rediscover your life's destiny and purpose. Do not grumble or complain; instead, pray earnestly to the God of Heaven, who is able hear your call and come down to rescue you.

The Sovereign Lord, the Restorer, and Redeemer of mankind, will water your dry places and cause your uncultivated and unfruitful life to spring forth like the lush green garden that it was meant to be. He is doing it for me and will complete the work that started the moment you were conceived in your mother's womb. You are born with and for a divine purpose in order to fulfill the mandate of God upon your life.

The Lord elevated my life to a platform where I am able to speak to men and women who are hurting, rejected, pushed aside, and left for dead. The one who did not have a voice, now, through the power of God, is able to prophesy, encourage, motivate and pray for those who have lost their voice and reason to live. There is a mighty comeback from all my setbacks, and I can only give glory and honour to my God for resurrecting me from the dead. When I was lost and undone, Jesus lifted me with His mighty hands; He holds me, never to let me go. It is a "But God" moment. Hallelujah!

ABOUT THE AUTHOR

 A writer, motivational speaker, counselor, trained teacher, and educator by profession, Mrs. Tretia Stewart-Angus is an ordained minister and pastor of Kingdom Encounter Ministry International. She preaches the undiluted Word of God, exhorts, motivates, and gives counsel to many. This astute woman of God is dedicated to her husband, Apostle Okino Angus, and is the mother of two beautiful girls, Theamoy and Justine. She is self-motivated and believes there is nothing that is impossible to achieve if you work hard, pray, and believe. Her guiding philosophy is entrenched in the Word of God, particularly Philippians 4:13, which says, "I can do all things through Christ who strengthens me."

Mrs. Tretia Stewart-Angus is a woman of grace and purpose who seeks to bring hope to battered and abused women and girls. Her passion is also to see young men and women rise above the horrors of their past and fulfill their God-given purpose.